REMEMBERING TOMMY

Tommy: a British infantryman pictured in c.1916. He carries full marching equipment, webbing, Short, Magazine, Lee–Enfield (SMLE) rifle, PH helmet gas mask in its haversack and steel helmet. A member of a pioneer battalion, he would have been expected to both fight and dig on the Western Front

REMEMBERING TOMMY

THE BRITISH SOLDIER IN THE FIRST WORLD WAR

PETER DOYLE & CHRIS FOSTER

The
History
Press

For all who served in 'Fred Karno's Army'

We are Fred Karno's Army
The ragtime infantry
We cannot march, we cannot shoot,
What bloody use are we?
And when we get to Berlin
The Kaiser he will say
Hoch! Hoch! Mein Gott,
What a bloody fine lot
Fred Karno's infantry

First published 2013
This paperback edition first published 2018

The History Press
The Mill, Brimscombe Port
Stroud, Gloucestershire, GL5 2QG
www.thehistorypress.co.uk

British Library Cataloguing in Publication Data.
A catalogue record for this book is available from the British Library.

ISBN 978 0 7509 8146 0

Typesetting and origination by The History Press
Printed in China

CONTENTS

REMEMBERING TOMMY

Tommy Atkins was the name first given to the British soldier by Wellington, but which stuck with him through two world wars. It had common currency on both sides of the line, 'Tommy' of the popular press becoming 'Tommee' shouted from the German lines. First appearing in official literature in 1815 (when it was used in *War Office Orders and Regulations*), the name also had a place a century later in the soldier's pay book of the Great War. Though the British soldier of 1914–18 saw himself as a member of 'Fred Karno's Army', an army of largely amateur soldiers more often than not muddling through the war, it is the name 'Tommy' that stuck. This familiar title became much more than a shorthand for the British soldier; it became imbued with concepts of unremitting stoicism, of phlegm and grim humour in the face of the extreme conditions of warfare. In more cynical times, these concepts might be fairly challenged, but the written word of the time, the letters, diaries and memoirs, all attest to its validity. And with the conditions of trench warfare so trying, it is now difficult for us to comprehend how they managed it. With all former combatants of that terrible war now gone, seeking out a means of understanding what it was like to serve requires us to delve into archives, to trawl through letters and diaries, and to listen to the

A soldier's memories

'What did you do in the war, Daddy?' A child's mementoes of the war

recorded words, fortunately captured by the nation's museums before it was too late.

And then there are the numerous artefacts, mostly everyday objects that might have been carried in the pack or pocket, or that might have sat on the table, draped an armchair or carried into the frontline. Often these were retained by a soldier because of an association with a time or place – a piece of trench art, a lighter used regularly, a uniform jacket hung in a wardrobe, a pay book kept as evidence of service – or sometimes they were preserved by chance, sat in a drawer or gathered in a forgotten corner. Each one has a hidden story, and each one provides the key to interpreting just a little of what was going on around the men and women of that war. And if each object has a story, then assembling them in context might assist us in our quest to understand just a bit more of what it was like to serve in this most significant period of history. As such, this book is a remembrance of Tommy Atkins, using the objects he might have carried, used and lived with throughout the four years of war. Soldiers are mostly absent from our pictures; the grouping of the artefacts and the situations they are placed in are there to stimulate the mind of the observer.

Our focus is both life at home and on the Western Front. Arguably, the Western Front was the most significant theatre of war, as it was here that the principal foe, Germany, would have to be beaten. Though at the time generals and politicians – divided into opposing camps of 'westerners' and 'easterners' – argued about the wisdom of either committing more men to the fields of northern Europe or opening and sustaining fronts (the so-called 'sideshows') in the Middle East and Balkans, it was France and Flanders that saw most of the British soldier.

On the Western Front, the British soldier expended prodigious efforts facing a determined enemy – an enemy equally determined to sit on the defensive in positions that represented the westernmost extent of a Greater Germany. Strong, and getting stronger, these entrenched positions were an inevitable consequence of the power of modern warfare, with artillery and the machine gun exacting a terrible price from attacking troops. The term 'Western Front' was borrowed from the Germans, who were fighting a war in both the east and west. It was here that a war of position developed in the winter of 1914, when the options for turning the flanks of the German armies advancing across France and Belgium like a 'swinging door' had been exhausted. From the moment that trenches had been dug it was inevitable that the war would descend into a war of trench lines and subterranean battles (as it had done in the Russo-Japanese War of 1904). Stretching from the Swiss frontier to the North Sea, these lines were inhabited by Allies from France, the British Empire and Belgium (ultimately joined in 1917–18 by the USA and the Portuguese). Though the British Army would take up a fraction of the whole line, its positions were an essential part of the Allied frontline throughout the war, with an increasing burden of responsibility as the war progressed. In the west, the Allied lines would be stretched in the face of offensives, yet they remained intact until 1918, when first the Germans, and then the Allies, were to break out of their positions, finally resuming open warfare in August 1918.

This book, then, takes a journey from the joining of the soldier through his tours of the trenches to his visits home – where domestic life on the home front carried on in the face of growing shortages and the threat of aerial attack. For space, it focuses on the period that encompasses the height of trench warfare, from early 1915 to late 1917, when life for the British soldier was dominated by a cycle of 'in the line–in reserves–in rest', each part composed of four to eight days on average. It is the infantryman who appears most in this book, as it was the infantryman who most experienced trench warfare during the war. But we cannot forget the large numbers of men who served the guns, who engineered the battlefield, and who supported the frontline soldiers. As such, the men of the artillery, engineers, Army Service Corps (ASC) and Royal Army Medical Corps (RAMC) also appear. In illustrating life at the front, we can only hint at the filth and degradation of the trenches, and cannot demonstrate fear, pain and suffering and loss – but the purpose of our book is to capture something of the atmosphere of the period. With objects mute witnesses to the events of wartime, placing them back in to context provides a key, unlocking just a fraction of the past. Our focus is on the routine of daily life; the unremarkable rather than the dramatic. The images allow observers to draw their own conclusions, and to conjure their own memories of family stories, of personal memoirs, of books read. In spirit, *Remembering Tommy* follows the rhythm illustrated by Pte Fergus Mackain, who, in a series of postcards, gave one of the most accurate depictions of the life of the average Tommy in existence.

Mackain had a deftness of touch in his charming and understated colour-washed cards. His cards, entitled *Sketches of Tommy's Life*, were published in France in four separate series of nine cards each (Imprimérie P. Gaulthier, Boulogne and Visé, Paris). The *Sketches*

Fergus Mackain, frontline infantryman and artist, manages to express what was uppermost in the thoughts of many soldiers – home

Fergus Mackain illustrates an artilleryman, 'somewhere in France'

themselves fall into four chapters of Tommy's Life: *In Training*; *At the Base*; *Up the Line*; and *Out on Rest*. Humorous aspects are present, of course, but underlying the cards is a deep understanding of what it was like to be a soldier on the Western Front. The soldier's kit is reproduced with minute detail: trench periscopes, bully beef tins, clasp knives, rifle pull-throughs, washing kit holdalls, webbing packs and helmets; these essential yet seemingly mundane items are reproduced in the background of the cards, and reward detailed inspection. Situations are apt, too – the seemingly endless issue of kit items; housey-housey at the base; issue of the rum ration and scanning the sky for trench mortars, whistle in hand in the trenches; ablutions in the reserve trenches – all are handled with an intimate understanding derived from direct experience.

This is understandable, after all: 4249 Private Fergus H.E. Mackain served with the 23rd (1st Sportsman's) Battalion Royal Fusiliers on the Western Front. The Sportsman's Battalion was raised in the autumn of 1914 by Mrs Cunliffe-Owen, a society lady sufficiently well connected to be able to telegraph Lord Kitchener with the question 'Will you accept complete battalion of upper and middle class men, physically fit, able to shoot and ride, up to the age of 45?' She was to receive the answer, 'Lord Kitchener gratefully accepts complete battalion.' Finally handed over to the army in April 1915, the 23rd Battalion was to serve in the 99th Brigade throughout the war, with 4,987 offic-

ers and men serving, and 3,241 as casualties – killed, wounded and missing. Mackain survived the war, serving with the battalion as a private and transferring to the Army Service Corps later in the war – as was usual with men who had suffered wounds and illness.

Mackain's story is not unusual, and his life as a private soldier undistinguished, but his cards are unique not simply because they illustrate the life of the average 'Tommy' in extraordinary detail. His cards often have Field Post Office stamps, and messages that draw attention to the similarities between the soldiers depicted on the cards, and the soldier sending the cards home. In this way, Mackain's cards act as windows on what life must have been like for the average soldier at the front, and are authentic documents of life in the Great War.

The British Empire fielded almost 9 million men, serving in all arms during the war. Of these, some 900,000 were killed – 10 per cent of the total – but a further 2 million were wounded, and almost 200,000 more were prisoners, or were reported missing. This means that over a third of the total were casualties in some form or other. For those who returned, many would put their memories behind them, others would proudly attend reunions and take an active part in remembrance. Very many would want to forget, and others, discharged as unfit, would live with the vestiges of war for the rest of their lives – all too short for some. This book is in remembrance of all those men who served with 'Fred Karno's Army'.

JOINING

Then the first war broke out and the early news of the invaders terrorising the women made me feel that must not happen here so I decided to enlist.

Pte Humphrey Mason, 6th Battalion, Oxfordshire and Buckinghamshire Light Infantry

GONE TO BE A SOLDIER

In the early stages of the war, within hours of its declaration, there was a flurry of activity in military circles. Regular soldiers were recalled from leave; reservists recalled to duty; Territorials called to the colours; and the ordinary civilian inspired by the spirit of the nation to join his country's forces. But the Great War was also to be the last hurrah for Britain's volunteer army. Prior to the conflict it had not been the 'British way' to maintain a mass standing army; instead, Britain's emphasis was on the recruitment of volunteers in times of crisis. Volunteers had been part of the army's structure since the mid part of the nineteenth century, with a clutch of rifle volunteers raised in 1859 in order to face the threats from the continent, France the persistent menace. These new battalions would outlive the threat from Napoleon III to form the backbone of the newly constructed Territorial Force, a direct outcome of the Haldane reforms of 1908. But battle experience would have to await the Boer War of 1899–1902, which provided some mettle, and some battle honours, to Britain's volunteer corps, with infantry and yeomanry cavalry battalions committed to the veldt. These now seasoned volunteer battalions would become integrated into the army's regimental system in

WHY AREN'T **YOU** IN KHAKI?
YOU'LL BE WANTED.
ENLIST AT ONCE.

The typical output of the Parliamentary Recruiting Committee, loaded with emotional blackmail

Britain's streets in 1914

1908. The 'Saturday night soldiers' of the Territorial volunteers, signed on with the commitment to regular parades at the local drill hall and a summer field camp, were to be Britain's home defence, becoming linked as battalions of the local county regiments – they would have no overseas obligation. That is, until war darkened the horizon.

So it was that when the Great War commenced, the infantry regiments each consisted of at least two regular battalions and two further Territorials in the United Kingdom. With Imperial commitments and

Home Defence duties, and with the expectation that the Royal Navy would be the bulwark of the nation, Britain could only commit six divisions to the field in support of France and its obligations towards the defence of Belgium. These professional soldiers became known as the 'Old Contemptibles', a term derived from an Imperial order issued by Kaiser Wilhelm II on 9 August: 'It is my Royal and Imperial command that you concentrate your energies, for the immediate present, upon one single purpose, and that is that you address all your skill and all the valour of my soldiers to exterminate first the treacherous English and walk over General French's contemptible little army.' These men, hard-pressed in the battles of 1914, would take the name on board with some pride. With the first of Britain's field armies comprising troops from regular battalions, and the second from those men of the Territorial battalions who volunteered for overseas service, Britain would have to consider its commitments.

With his breadth of experience in the Victorian 'small wars' and his actions in South Africa, Field Marshal Lord Kitchener was an obvious choice as a war leader. With Field Marshal Sir John French commander-in-chief in the field, Kitchener was summoned to the War Office to take on the direction of the war and to take a seat in the Cabinet. With little political experience and a strong-minded personality,

Recruiting posters were intended to remind men of their patriotic duty

Sketches
of Tommy's life
In Training. — N° 1

" That seems to mean me all right "

Posted in streets, billboards and public places, recruiting posters had a major impact in 1914–15

Kitchener was difficult to influence, and more often than not unwilling to give up even the most trifling of actions to his staff. But he had foresight at this stage of the war that was not shared by any other: this new European War would be costly in manpower, and would last at least three years. It would not be over by Christmas. Impatient with the current recruiting system, and in the knowledge that maintaining an adequate flow of soldiers to the front would be of great importance, the Secretary of State for War made a direct appeal to the public for more men. The first appeal was for 100,000 men, a campaign that would be driven by his own image pasted up on billboards and recruiting offices.

To assist Kitchener in his work, the Parliamentary Recruiting Committee (PRC) was formed in August 1914, a cross-party body administered by officers of the major political parties. Senior representatives of the Liberal and Unionist parties worked hard at developing means of persuading their fellow men to join the colours. With public meetings and a flurry of posters (though not strictly involving the issue of Kitchener's famous pointing finger), the PRC became an active body that would ensure that Britain was united in sending its men as quickly to the front as possible.

The 'First Hundred Thousand' (K1) were recruited within days of Kitchener's appeal, and the War Minister was to issue four further appeals through the late summer and early autumn of 1914. Recruiting offices sprang up across the country, with local municipal buildings and mobile recruiting offices pressed into service, usually bedecked with banners and posters. Would-be soldiers were given the briefest of medicals before being formally 'attested' as Soldiers of the King. Queues formed outside well-founded or hastily contrived recruiting offices up and down the country, with a crush of men waiting to 'sign on' and receive their first symbolic wages, the King's Shilling binding them to military service.

The government recognised that married men of recruiting age might need financial inducement to leave their families: separation allowances for an average married private were paid at a weekly rate of 12s 6d for a wife alone, 17s 6d for a wife and one child, 21s for a wife and two children, and so on. But this took into account a compulsory 'allotment' of money from the soldier's own wages – of 6d a day (half the basic shilling a day earned by privates without other enhancements). Those soldiers with other 'dependants' – that is, 'any person who is found as a fact to have been dependent on the soldier ... to whom the soldier is bound by some natural tie' – would also need help. In such cases, the government pledged to make up the amount lost to the dependant by the soldier having joined the army – after the appropriate deductions, of course. How important these factors were in influencing soldiers to join up is a moot point. For many middle-class men, further enticement might be the opportunity to return to a good job with a decent employer after the war. Some employers went out of their way to support their employee recruits: not only would their positions be held open, but they would also receive other benefits such as support of the family in some way, or the periodic sending of 'comforts' to the frontline.

Initial recruitment to Kitchener's Army was steady if unspectacular – though it was significantly boosted in the aftermath of the British retreat from Mons in August 1914. The men of K1, K2 and so on took their places in the ranks of the existing army system, but very soon energetic and influential individuals were forming whole battalions: men intended to train together and serve together. The concept was born

Above: Recruits attesting as Soldiers of the King, 1914

Right: Signing the attestation certificate. Recruits promised to serve for the 'duration of the war'

following a request from the City of London to raise a whole battalion of 'stockbrokers' in August 1914. But the proliferation of the concept was in large part due to the action of Lord Derby, the so-called 'King of Lancashire', who introduced the notion that men of the 'commercial classes' might wish to serve their country in a battalion of their comrades, their 'pals'. The 'Liverpool Pals' was the result. The implication was that middle-class men would not be forced to serve alongside men they would neither know nor understand: men of 'lower social class'. Based on the snobbery of the time, it was a resounding success – though it would lead ultimately to the decimation of local communities. In the end, it was these men who would contribute to the much-debated 'lost generation', men of all walks of life who 'answered the call' to be decimated on the Somme in July 1916.

Men from Kitchener's Army came from all walks of life: the cottage kitchen of a Manchester Pal

*Opposite: An officer's
cap of the Durham Light
Infantry. Early in the war,
officers still carried a
sword, the 1897 infantry
pattern. It was soon
discarded in the trenches*

An avalanche of 'City' and 'Pals' battalions were formed from men with similar backgrounds and circumstances, the concept spreading like wildfire throughout the industrial north and Midlands. Becoming a matter of civic pride, each battalion was raised by local dignitaries, who fed, clothed and equipped it until the unit was taken over by the War Office. Only then would the costs of raising the battalion be met by the government, as it became a Service Battalion (numbered in sequence after the Territorials) of the County Regiment. Initially, recruits were more often than not clothed in civilian garb (or a strange mix of civilian clothing and military uniform),

and as training camps had not yet been formed or established, Kitchener's men found themselves still living at home. As a stopgap, simple uniforms were supplied in what has become known as 'Kitchener Blue' – blue serge in place of khaki; men looked like postmen or tram conductors. Recruitment snowballed, reaching 1,186,357 by the end of 1914.

The flow of men to the colours continued almost unabated throughout 1914 and into 1915 – and particularly when the liner RMS *Lusitania* was sunk with great loss of life, and to great public outrage. Yet with the initial rush of men to join the colours in the early stages of the war, it was inevitable that there would

*A corporal of the
Manchester Regiment
poses with his friends*

be others less keen, men who ran the risk while in civilian clothing of approbation from the female vigilantes of the 'Order of the White Feather'.

Founded in 1914 by Admiral Charles Fitzgerald and author Mary Ward, the 'Order' persuaded women to present men who were not in uniform with the device – a traditional badge of cowardice – though this might include wounded, off-duty or on-leave soldiers and sailors. Despite these actions, recruitment took a sharp dip in 1915, declining month-on-month from its peak in August 1914. If Britain was to preserve its contribution to the war effort, then action to stop the fall was urgently needed. Lord Derby was appointed 'director of recruitment' in October 1915 to address this decline; the calls for compulsion were getting louder.

The first steps to compulsion had, in fact, already been taken, with the National Registration Act of July 1915. The Act required every citizen between the ages of 15 and 65 to register their name, place of residence, nature of work and other details, and receive a National Registration Card. By October 1915 there were 21,627,596 names on the register, of which 5,158,211 were men of military age. Of this figure, 1,519,432 men were identified as being in reserved occupations, vital to the war effort. Under National Registration men exempted from military service became known as 'starred', from the black star that was added against their names on the official records. The engineering trades unions had been made responsible for identifying and exempting skilled men from military service, issuing their member with Trade Cards. All would wear 'On War Service' badges (first granted to men working under Admiralty orders in 1914, and later expanded to more workers in 1915) and carry 'protection certificates' – protecting them from the white feather.

Kitchener's Army, Kitchener Blue, 6th Battalion, Oxfordshire and Buckinghamshire Light Infantry. Two sets of father and sons in the same battalion, September 1914. Corporal B.W. Mason (far right) and Private H.N.T. Mason (second from right). Both survived the war

The rag-tag Kitchener's Army (6th Battalion, Oxfordshire and Buckinghamshire Light Infantry), wearing a mixture of civilian and military clothes. Corporal Mason is second from the left (standing); his son, Private Mason, is second from the left (middle row)

NEW
WINDOW DISPLAY
COMING SOON

Military headgear in a
haberdasher's shop, c.1914

*Above: Recruitment in
1914–15 had peaks and
troughs; the sinking of the
Lusitania in May 1915 saw a
resurgence in the numbers
of men joining*

*Left: 'The Huns carry out
their threat to murder'*

*Opposite: The white
feather was the badge
of cowardice and was
presented to unwitting
men in civilian clothes,
up and down the country*

Above: Men exempted from military service wore 'On War Service' badges to help them avoid the 'Order of the White Feather'

Right: War worker 'On War Service', c.1915

Left: Men voluntarily attested under the 'Derby Scheme' wore a khaki armband

National Registration identified that there were at least 3.4 million men who were technically able to join the forces, but by the autumn of 1915 the numbers actually joining was falling at an alarming rate, not sufficient to fulfil the requirement of 35,000 men per week envisaged by Lord Kitchener. Lord Derby drew up a scheme that would force the issue. The 'Derby Scheme' proposed the voluntary attestation (an agreement under oath, a solemn and legal undertaking to join the colours when called to them) of all men between 18 and 40, with men of the same age and marital status being grouped together to be called to the colours in batches. Central to the scheme was the promise that younger, unmarried men would be the first in line, and that married men would be last to go. Lord Derby invited all eligible men to attest by 15 December 1915: over 2 million of the 3.5 million men available for military service failed to attest. With this last-ditch act, Lord Derby had effectively paved the way to compulsory service; there could be few legitimate claims to the contrary if Britain was to succeed in its war aims.

With the failure of Derby's scheme, compulsion to join came with the Military Service Act of January 1916. Now, all fit single men between the ages of 18 and 41 would be compelled to join the colours, married men joining them in the second Military Service Act of May 1916. Unfit men were exempted for the time being but three further Acts, in April 1917, January 1918 and April 1918, would find ways of 'combing out' more men for military service (the last reducing the recruitment age to 17, while, at the same time, increasing it to 55). Each man called to the colours was required to attend a compulsory medical that would test physical attributes, height (5ft 4in initially, with a chest expansion of up to 34in), general fitness, eyesight and dental status. With many men's health faring badly in the industrial cities of the British Empire, a number would be rejected, and the formal categories of fitness to serve, from A1 (fit) to CIII (fit only for home service), came into common currency as slang for anything 'good' or 'worn out'.

Dear Win
Just to let you know, I was examined yesterday after waiting 6 hours. Hot stuff arn't they. Well they have rejected me. I have not been passed for any branch of Service. Ta Ta, Love F.S.

Postcard to Win Dellow, North London, 1916

With compulsion came refusal; conscientious objectors – COs or 'conchies' – were those who objected to military service due to their deep-held beliefs that war was wrong. Under the Military Service Acts, conscientious objectors had to sit before a tribunal to determine their case on an individual basis. Those holding the most fundamental objections refused to engage in any work, civilian or military, which might support the prosecution of the war. The tribunals set up to explore these objections were difficult and challenging, and men were subjected to brutal

questioning. For these men, the alternative to military service could be a long spell in prison 'with hard labour' for refusing to wear the king's uniform in 1916; those willing to serve in the Non Combatant Corps, working away from the front, would find their labour hard, with their officers and NCOs retained from the Provost Corps – the army's prison service. COs would be poorly treated by all.

The development of what was to become Britain's largest citizen army continued throughout the war, with four distinct and separate components. The regulars formed the first of Britain's Great War armies: regular soldiers who had served in the first two battalions of an infantry regiment in the pre-war period, alternating between them on home or overseas service in one of Britain's Imperial outposts. Sent to France in 1914–15, they became the 'Old Contemptibles', the small professional army committed to stemming the flow of the German tide across France. Britain's second line, the Territorials, or 'terriers', were intended as home defence: organised into Territorial Divisions, they would be committed overseas if they had taken the 'Imperial Service Obligation' waiving their rights to home service alone – these 'First Line' Territorial Divisions were committed to battle in 1915.

The Battalion has volunteered for foreign service, and will go as a battalion. Eighty per cent volunteered, and of the remaining 20 per cent some have applied for commissions. We have started recruiting again to fill up from 800 to 1,000, so as to go at full strength.

Pte D.H. Bell, London Rifle Brigade, 28 August 1914

Those men who did not volunteer for overseas service were transferred to 'Second Line' Territorial battalions, but they too would be organised into divisions and, in 1916, with the introduction of conscription, they would also ultimately serve abroad.

For Field Marshal Sir John French, commander-in-chief of the British Expeditionary Force (BEF) in 1915, fighting a war effectively meant both men and munitions, and his hope was that he could hold off until both arrived. The creation of the Ministry of Munitions would provide the weapons; the mass of men would come from Kitchener's Army in training across Britain, ready to deliver on its promise in 1916. But with this New Army depleted on the rusting barbed wire of the Somme and Flanders in 1916–17, it was actually the final men to join the colours, the conscripts of 1917–18, who would be the ones to drive back the Germans, to break through the Hindenberg Line, and to carry a huge number of casualties. It would fall to them to win the war. Not many would last the whole course.

I could go on for hours detailing instances of exceptional escapes from injury and death from shellfire, bombs and mines. I seemed to have some special form of protection. I know I carried the lucky fourpenny piece but there was something really deep; was it mother's prayers?

Pte Humphrey Mason, Kitchener volunteer, 6th Battalion, Oxfordshire and Buckinghamshire Light Infantry

Opposite: In the parlour: patriotic songs on the harmonium; 'It's a Long Way to Tipperary' became the song of the war and was much parodied at the front; at home, it was difficult to escape from the war

Memories of a soldier. Cap badges were common gifts from soldiers leaving for the front

Leaving for the front

EQUIPPING THE SOLDIER

Opposite: Khaki Service Dress, worn by father and son, Corporal B.W. Mason (left) and Private H.N.T. Mason (right), 6th Battalion, Oxfordshire and Buckinghamshire Light Infantry

Below: Kitchener's men leaving for their training camp, September 1914

For all of these men, enlistment meant being kitted out as a soldier, the discomfort of the transition from civilian life, and intensive training before going overseas for the long trail to the front. For the regulars and Territorials, supply of uniforms and equipment was less of a problem than it was to prove to be for Kitchener's Army. Regular troops based at their traditional depots had well-established supply chains and efficient quartermasters,

while the Territorials were equipped by local Territorial Associations deliberately set up to see to their every need – often supplying distinctly different uniforms and equipment from their regular colleagues, deemed suitable for home service. For the newly formed Kitchener's Army it was a different story altogether. With a relatively small number of clothing companies servicing the British Army's peacetime needs, an influx

UPPER WHARFEDALE RECRUITS LEAVING GRASSINGTON STATION SEPT. 21. 1914.

of thousands of men put severe strains on the supply system, especially with the raising of whole battalions by civic dignitaries, who took on the responsibility to equip their men before they were formally 'handed over' to the army. To meet the needs of the new armies, civilian contractors were employed to produce the uniforms necessary, and many more were derived from overseas, the USA in particular. With the supply of khaki serge strained, blue serge was used in its place. First issued in any quantity in September 1914, this created the uniform style that quickly became known as 'Kitchener Blue'. In many cases, would-be soldiers would wear a rag-tag of civilian clothing, Kitchener Blue, and odds and ends such as puttees, intended to create some kind of military look. Quartermasters were hard-pressed to meet their requirements.

The khaki uniform worn by the troops was first developed in 1902 as a replacement for the traditional red coat of the British infantryman. Although still in service in action during the Zulu War of 1879, the need for something more suited to modern warfare than a red coat was learned in India and the Afghan Wars, with the development of a uniform in a less conspicuous dun colour: khaki. A term linked to Tommy's Imperial service, it was derived from the Hindi-Urdu word for dust or mud-covered. A cotton service dress of khaki was in full use in the Boer War of 1899–1902, and this led to the development of the wool serge version used by Tommy in the First World War. The 1902 Service Dress was the product of a basic military requirement to have a comfortable and serviceable uniform that would be suited for field conditions, in all weathers. This wool serge uniform went through several modifications in the 'Lists of Changes' issued periodically by the War Office, but by 1914 had settled down to a pattern that was used more or less throughout the war.

Sketches
of Tommy's life

In Training. — Nº 2

It's funny how rotten your first uniform looks on you. You wonder how the
other chaps manage to appear so smart.

F. Mackain

*Finding the correct
fit was often a
difficult proposition*

The wartime Service Dress tunic was characteristically loose fitting (if it fitted at all – a fact not lost on Fergus Mackain), with a turned-down collar, patches at the shoulder to bear the extra wear from the position of the rifle butt in action, and pleats to the rear of the jacket. It had a pair of box-pleated patch pockets with button-down flaps at the upper chest, and a pair of deep pockets let into the tunic skirt, again with button-down flaps. A simple pocket was also sewn into the inside right skirt of the tunic to take the soldier's first field dressing – the emergency bandages carried by all soldiers on active service. Two brass hooks, often removed or lost through use, were intended to support the belt in its correct position between the sixth and seventh tunic button. For the most part, these buttons were simple brass buttons – known as General Service or 'GS' buttons – bearing the royal arms. Some regiments insisted upon men buying and replacing these with regimental-patterned examples. The jackets of 'rifle' regiments in particular were distinguished by black horn buttons bearing a bugle; so distinctive were these that the men were often referred to by others as 'black button bastards'. Shoulder straps bore regimental insignia in the form of brass shoulder titles, but a range of other insignia were also used. Throughout the war, insignia were added to the sleeves, including rank badges, specialist trade and appointment badges, and divisional insignia.

In late 1915, with the War Office suffering the pressure of large numbers of men coming into the army, a simplified version of the Service Dress was introduced, intended to reduce the time taken to manufacture it. Possessing none of the refinements of the original, it was even more shapeless, and dispensed with the rifle patches at the shoulders, the pocket box pleats, the rear fitting pleats to the tunic, and the brass belt hooks. This was never in favour and, although worn throughout the war, it was replaced with the standard 1902 pattern as soon as was practical.

Both types of Service Dress were worn in the trenches: the woollen jackets, warm but rough, were intended to be worn over a series of layers. Starting with woollen underwear and a long flannel shirt, in cold weather the jacket was worn over a woollen cardigan – officially issued but often replaced or added to by the actions of knitters at home who served to create knitted garments during the bitter winters. Woollen mufflers, socks, balaclava helmets and a host of other small items also became the staple of many parcels bound for the front.

Held up by braces or a belt (belts often personalised by the soldier with the addition of cap badges or buttons), the Service Dress trousers worn by the average soldier were quite close fitting, with a narrow leg designed to be worn with puttees to provide the required military silhouette; mounted soldiers wore breeches. Puttees were derived, like the khaki service dress, from the British experience in India: the term 'puttee' originated from another Hindi word (this time, appropriately enough, meaning bandage). Perhaps intended to provide a covering for the lower leg that would give greater support and protection,

or perhaps just a military fashion of the day, puttees were used by most nations during the war. Learning how to tie the puttee soon became a badge of the experienced soldier. Consisting of long wool serge strips supplied with cotton tapes, puttees were wound around the leg from the ankle to the knee for the average infantryman. Mounted soldiers (including cavalrymen, artillerymen and Army Service Corps men, amongst others) were distinguished by their practice of winding the puttee from the knee to the ankle, the tapes wound close to the latter. As a way of expressing their own personality, soldiers would also create, using judiciously applied folds, fancy patterns with their puttees.

According to the weekly *Illustrated War News* of February 1916, the traditional East Midlands centre of shoemaking, Northampton, was to be stretched

The wool flannel shirt and cardigan worn under the uniform jacket

Opposite: Service Dress jacket, cap and swagger stick of a sergeant in the Post Office Rifles, a London Regiment Battalion that wore black horn buttons

Soldier of the Rifle Brigade, c.1915

Right: Soldier of the Duke of Wellington's Regiment (West Riding), wearing Light Machine Gunner (LG) and Gun Layer (L) proficiency badges on his sleeve. As an infantryman, he wound his puttees from ankle to knee

Below: Corporal David Hepworth, Army Service Corps. As a mounted soldier, he wore breeches and wound his puttees from knee to ankle

to capacity in supplying boots; not only for the British Army, but also for most of the Allies in the field, employed on all fronts. During peacetime alone, some 245,000 pairs of boots were required annually to supply the British Army. The 'Regulation' British field boot for most of the war was roughly square-toed, produced in thick hide with the rough side out. Soldiers issued with the boots for field use were instructed to pack the rough leather with dubbin in order to create a more water-resistant material, and this produced the tan colour that is so typical of the field boot. The standard pattern early in the war was the B2 (first introduced in 1913); the later B5 boot, distinguished by its distinctive quarters and copper rivet, saw widespread introduction in 1915–16. Other footwear used by Tommy on the Western Front would be the high boot of the mounted artilleryman, and the so-called 'trench waders', made by the North British Rubber Company in Scotland, and centrally held as 'trench stores'.

In 1914, British soldiers went to war in headgear that was to provide an element of military smartness, a peaked cap that was adopted in 1905. This was not designed to protect the head from anything other than the elements, and had a stiffened rim and peak, bearing the traditional cap badges of the British Army. The stiffness of this headgear made it awkward and so in late 1914, in answer to the impracticality of this headgear was the issue of the winter Service Dress cap, which was well padded and equipped with flaps to keep the ears warm. Ungainly, the mythology is that this cap, which became known as a 'gor'blimey', was so nicknamed by the first sergeant major who cast his eyes upon one – the term deriving from cockney slang for 'God blind me'. Both stiff and winter Service Dress caps became superseded once the steel helmet was first issued, towards the close of

Standard issue B5 boots

1915. With the arrival of the steel helmet, a new soft and practical cap was issued in March 1916 that was capable of being folded and stowed in the soldier's equipment, as it had no stiff components. A stitched peak was the only concession to smartness, and Tommy often personalised it by plaiting the leather strap, while parting the strap components was also popular. A final modification was the issue of a denim version in 1918.

With the profile of most British soldiers looking broadly the same throughout the war, it was left to the Scots to cut a dash with their distinctive form

British soldier of the Royal Engineers, c.1914, with stiff 1905 pattern cap and Victorian Slade Wallace pattern belt

Clockwise from left: Winter Service Dress cap (gor'blimey) and simplified Service Dress jacket; gor'blimey cap worn by a sergeant of the Royal Engineers, who also wears a short warm coat issued to mounted soldiers; the stiff-peaked 1905 pattern cap, worn in this case with an officer's bronzed cap badge of the Royal Sussex Regiment

Opposite: Uniform of a staff sergeant in the Army Service Corps, with the soft Service Dress cap

Left: Uniform of a staff sergeant in the Royal Field Artillery, with spurs and 1903 pattern leather bandolier, plus the denim soft Service Dress cap

Below left: Soldier of the Royal Field Artillery, equipped with soft Service Dress cap and bandolier, c.1917

Men often braided the chinstraps of their caps, as with this soldier of the Middlesex Regiment

cloth. The Scottish Service Dress (SD) jacket was also special – its front skirts were cut back in the manner of a traditional doublet to allow the wearing of the full-dress sporran – in Private Dennis' case by the simple expedient of cutting the corners off his standard SD tunic.

To complement the appearance of the highland soldier, there were a range of caps and bonnets. Early war, the commonest was the glengarry, found in a variety of patterns: plain dark blue with a red tuft or 'tourie' (worn by the Black Watch and Cameron Highlanders); rifle green with a black tourie (the Cameronians and Highland Light Infantry); red-and-white diced border and red tourie (Argyll and Sutherland Highlanders); and finally red-green-white diced borders with red tourie (Royal Scots, Royal Scots Fusiliers, King's Own Scottish Borderers, Seaforths and Gordons). There were other regiments who adopted the glengarry too: the Territorial 10th Battalion of the King's Liverpool Regiment – the Liverpool Scottish – wore the red-white-green diced border, while the Kitchener's Army battalions of the Northumberland Fusiliers, known as the Tyneside Scottish, adopted a plain black glengarry with red tourie and black silk rosette. There were other variants, too. Impractical in the field, the glengarry would be replaced in 1915 by first the beret-like Balmoral bonnet, and then the serge khaki Tam O'Shanter bonnet, a large, circular but otherwise shapeless object that nonetheless distinguished the Scot.

While the ordinary soldier was issued with his uniform, it was incumbent upon the officer to provide his own. As this was paid for from their own pockets, it was not surprising that some officers found it difficult, even though grants were available (initially £20 in August 1914, but soon rising to £50 at the

of highland dress. Many Scottish regiments were kilted, a dress distinction that was always popular with onlookers and which was worn with pride by the 'kilties' themselves. According to Private Dennis, transferred from an English rifle regiment to the Cameron Highlanders, the kilt was warm to wear with its many folds of woollen tartan, the downside of the folds being their propensity to harbour lice, as well as their ability to soak up vast amounts of water, adding to the weight burden of the average soldier. The bright colours of some regimental tartans were also a problem, such that, by 1915, the kilt was to be covered by a simple apron of khaki

Left: Sergeant in the Gordon Highlanders, with cut-away Service Dress, and kilt apron

Below: Two soldiers of the Liverpool Scottish, 1915

Right: Scots soldiers wearing Tam O'Shanter bonnets and carrying SMLE rifles

Below: Soldier of the London Scottish, c.1915, a battalion distinguished by its plain-weave, Hodden Grey kilt

end of the year, as prices rose in what became a competitive market for limited supplies). For the new officer, obtaining his kit also was fraught with confusion, particularly with most of the larger stores in London and elsewhere offering to supply complete kits (uniform, Sam Browne belt equipment, compass, whistle, revolver, field glasses and so on) to new officers.

Kit hasn't arrived yet: the revolver has, however, a most deadly weapon. The sword, a claymore, is coming in a day or two. As regards the 'tash' I can just get hold of it nicely now and so coax it into a twirly growth.

2nd Lt Christopher Wilkinson Brown, 3rd Battalion, Royal Scots Fusiliers, Fort Matilda, Greenock, 12 September 1914

Glengarry and other items of a soldier in the Gordon Highlanders: Private David Deas, a cabinet maker from Lancaster who, after receiving wounds in his head and leg, was medically downgraded and transferred to the Labour Corps

The expense was considerable, and making the wrong choices was common – particularly when the purchaser was tempted to add so-called trench gadgets, and when the colonel was particularly strict in his application of dress code. Shirts, ties, breeches even, would be subject to scrutiny; getting the correct shade, a challenge. Newly minted officers were all too easy to distinguish from their 'active service' comrades.

He was the 'man from the front.' And I noticed with secret misgivings that he had not removed the badges of rank from his arm, or sewed his two stars upon his shoulder-straps; he had not removed his bright buttons, and substituted them for leather ones such as are worn on golfing jackets; and in his valise, he told us, he had his Sam Browne belt.

Lt B. Adams, Royal Welsh Fusiliers, 1915

Officers' Service Dress allowed the uninitiated to distinguish the rank of the wearer easily; so easily, in fact, that at the front it was to provide enemy snipers something clear to aim at. Tailored to the needs of the individual officer, the Service Dress jacket nevertheless had to conform to the standard sealed pattern, having four buttons of regimental, rather than general service, pattern; an open step-down collar to be worn with regulation shirt and tie (the original 1902 pattern specification was for a closed stand and fall collar, sometimes used in the war); and a wide skirt with voluminous patch pockets. The collar bore a pair of distinctive collar badges, usually bronzed; cap badges were also bronzed. Badges of rank were generally applied to the cuffs of the tunic in a distinctive manner; easy to spot by the discerning sniper. Some officers took it upon themselves to move these badges to the shoulder straps, an affectation that had always been used by the Guards. Known as 'wind-up' tunics, the implication of this name was the reasonable fact that the alteration was made in order to make the jacket less conspicuous. Later in the war, many jackets were tailored like this from scratch.

The officer's jacket was worn with breeches of Bedford cord and a variety, according to personal taste, of footwear – from polished riding top boots and high laced 'trench boots' to simple brown ankle boots and puttees. Officers' puttees, almost invariably made by Fox's, were distinguished by their identification of a left and right puttee through the expedient of applying a small button, marked 'L' and 'R', to the relevant one. The officer's cap was similarly tailor-made, with a short peak and narrow chinstrap, often padded for warmth, and very quickly battered to give that 'active service' look. So-called 'trench' versions had a fold-down flap that fastened to the front of the cap, intended, like the soldiers' gor'blimey, to be proof against poor weather.

The standard cold weather protection issued to the average soldier was the greatcoat: a cumbersome wool serge coat, with a single row of brass GS buttons that weighed in at around 6lb, a considerable amount, even when dry. Expensive to manufacture, the greatcoat was also a hefty responsibility for the average soldier, who was expected to look after it – on pain of being fined a significant sum of money. Difficult to wear with equipment, and prone to fouling with mud and water – creating an even weightier piece of clothing – the greatcoat was bulky and long, its flaps coming to resemble slabs of mud as soldiers moved through the trenches. The mounted pattern was shorter, and more favoured; the average Tommy in the winter trenches was tempted to cut down his coat accordingly, to prevent its skirts trailing in the mud.

In fact, greatcoats were more often left with the large pack, or 'valise', with the battalion transport, with other means of keeping the body core warm provided. The first of these was the outlandish (and multicoloured) goatskin sleeveless jerkin issued in

2nd Lieut. H. de B. Cordes. M.C. Scots Guards.

Opposite: Officer of the Royal Field Artillery, with Sam Browne belt, sword and spurs, c.1914

Below: 2nd Lieutenant Hugh de Bary Cordes MC, Scots Guards, who died in France, 27 September 1918, aged 19

late 1914 that was to see action well into 1916. Worn with the fur out, these malodorous garments were nevertheless a means of keeping the trunk warm. Goatskins were replaced from 1915 onwards with hard-wearing sleeveless leather jerkins, lined with wool serge and having leather 'football' buttons. Worn either over or under the tunic, these provided warmth and protection, and were much favoured. Protection from the wet weather of Flanders was, at first, through the groundsheet, and from 1917 onwards by the innovation of a groundsheet that could be buttoned up to the neck to provide a cape. Officers, providing their own uniform, had greater freedom of choice in their outerwear. They too mostly adopted short coats, the double-breasted wool 'British Warm' being a favourite; or alternatively the lightweight 'Trench Coat' by Burberry, Aquascutum and a host of other manufacturers.

Right: 'Wind-up' jacket worn by Lieutenant Edward William Seymour of the 3rd Battalion, Grenadier Guards, at the crossing of the Broembeek, part of the Third Battle of Ypres, October 1917; an ordinary soldier's jacket, it has rank stars on its shoulder straps. Lieutenant Seymour survived the war, after being wounded in March 1918

Opposite: Soldier of the King's (Liverpool) Regiment, wearing stiff cap and 'dismounted pattern' greatcoat

With quartermasters having difficulties supplying the uniform needs of a greatly expanded army, it is not surprising that they were faced with an even bigger crisis when it came to military equipment. At the very least, soldiers could train in any clothing they had available – but to learn how to fight and move like a soldier under a great variety of conditions meant that they had to have access to their equipment. With the supply of webbing a matter of some importance to the army, severe strains started to tell upon the supply chain, especially as there were only two companies capable of producing the equipment sets in the country. Through the use of civilian clothing, manufacturers and overseas imports resolved many of the difficulties of uniform supplies to the expanded army: the supply of load-bearing equipment could not be fixed so easily. In many cases, soldiers would have to make do with what was available: obsolete or dummy rifles, equipment sets extemporised from outdated stocks. In addition, the War Office commissioned a set of equipment in leather that was based upon the basic format of the webbing, but which was quicker to manufacture, and easier to source from overseas manufacturers. Large orders were placed – but the first sets of Pattern 1914 equipment were not available until months after the soldiers concerned had received their uniforms, not an ideal situation for a completely novice army.

The provision of appropriate load-bearing equipment has been a question that has taxed the military mind every since the infantryman was first conceived. For centuries, the design of equipment – to include ammunition carriers, haversacks for accoutrements, ration carriers, and so on – has centred on the belt, with shoulder straps and braces designed to spread the weight. British equipment, however, employed

Drivers of the Army Service Corps wearing sheepskin-lined coats. Private Bill Pratt, who came back from France, stands to the right

Part of the success of the 1908 pattern equipment set lay with one of its greatest innovations; designed by Major Burrowes of the Royal Irish Fusiliers in 1906, it was a complete 'system'. Its thick woven cotton strapping (invented by the Mills equipment company in the United States in the late nineteenth century) also had many advantages over leather, which was difficult to keep clean, and was cumbersome and liable to stretch when wet. The 1908 set consisted of belt, cross-straps, left and right cartridge carriers (designed to carry 150 rounds in ten pouches, each holding three five-round chargers), water bottle, entrenching tool head carrier and bayonet frog. Innovatively, the wooden handle, or helve, for the entrenching tool was strapped to the scabbard of the bayonet. In addition, there was a small haversack, and large pack, with cross-straps to keep the pack in place and balanced. Unlike many of its contemporaries, which tended to load the belt and put strain on the lower back of the soldier, the 1908 equipment also possessed additional straps behind the cartridge carriers that helped distribute their weight more evenly, some of the load being taken up by the shoulder straps. The equipment could be taken off like a jacket, and on the march the 3in-wide belt could be unbuckled for comfort. Originally, the stud fastenings for the ammunition pouches matched on both left- and right-hand carriers, but this was soon changed in 1914 when it was found that ammunition was being lost from the left-hand version, and additional straps were added. Later in the war, and as an economy measure, the press-studs were replaced by post and hole fasteners.

With the influx of a huge number of men into the armed forces at the beginning of the Great War, the Mills Equipment Company was seriously overstretched – it simply could not meet the demand placed upon it to supply regular, Territorial and service

a more equable system of weight distribution, a collaboration of military ideas and manufacturing innovation, and it was the set known as the Pattern 1908 Web Infantry Equipment that was the ideal: the official guide praised its versatility, its balance, its flexibility, and its lack of constricting chest straps. All of these made the equipment special, which meant that soldiers would discard other patterns in its favour, wherever possible.

Above: The 1908 pattern webbing, showing the complex system of supporting straps

Left: A fully equipped soldier of the Essex Regiment at a camp in England, wearing 1908 pattern webbing and carrying a SMLE rifle

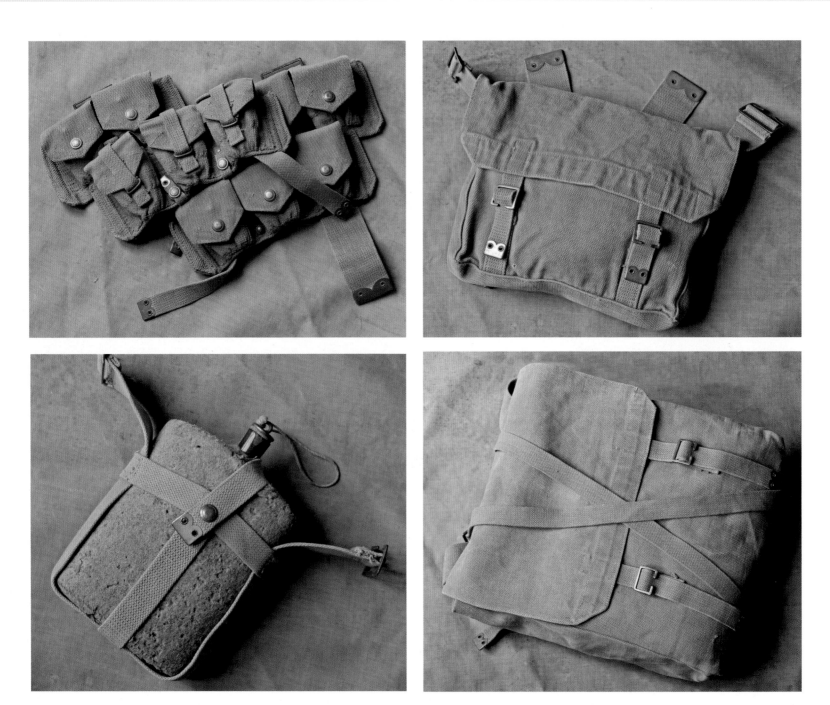

Clockwise from top left: left and right cartridge carriers of the 1908 set; the haversack of the 1908 pattern set; large pack or valise; water bottle and cradle. The equipment has been 'blancoed', a paste-like cleaner that gave a uniform green colour

battalions with sufficient webbing equipment sets. As such, a stopgap was needed, one that would do the same job but which could be manufactured from leather – which, despite its many deficiencies, was freely available. As such, the Pattern 1914 equipment was designed, based on the Mills-Burrowes webbing. Although using webbing for haversack and large pack, it employed leather for waist belt, cross-straps, cartridge carriers, entrenching tool holder, bayonet frog and water bottle cradle. The belt used a snake and hook fastener, inherited from nineteenth-century belt patterns, and a convenient hole in the leather backing to this fastener allowed the belt to be extended on the march. The Pattern 1914 cartridge carriers were made as simple pouches, designed to take a cotton bandolier holding fifty cartridges in five-round chargers – 100 rounds in all, and therefore fifty rounds fewer than the original. The resulting set was serviceable, but less efficient at distributing weight than the original webbing, and was almost exclusively issued to Service Battalions. The sets were manufactured in the UK and in the United States, with varying quality, and consisted of brown marbled leather, in some cases dyed green. In a few battalions, the leather equipment was ultimately discarded in favour of webbing salvaged from the battlefield, or from field hospitals.

As with all officers' kit, load-bearing equipment was privately purchased, although conforming to regulations. It was based around the Sam Browne belt – typically with a single cross-strap, but sometimes with double straps. In the early war period, the belt usually supported the sword frog (soon discarded), the service revolver in a leather holster, an ammunition pouch, a canvas haversack and waterproof cotton map case and message pad. Separate from these, carried by a fully laden officer

Below top: The 1907 pattern sword bayonet with attachment for the wooden handle, or helve, of the entrenching tool

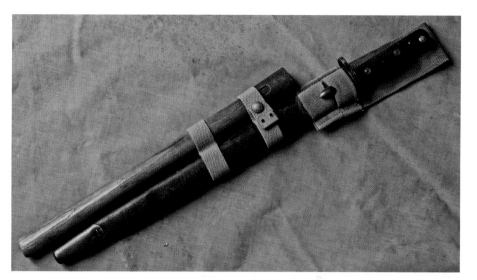

Below bottom: Entrenching tool and webbing carrier

using leather cross-straps, was a vernier compass in leather case, water bottle, and binoculars – the latter notoriously difficult to source, since most were made in Germany pre-war. A walking stick ('ash plant') was also *de rigueur*. The usual sidearm carried by an officer was a .455 calibre Webley revolver. The Mark VI was first introduced in May 1915, and became the most common service revolver used by the end of the war. It was cumbersome and difficult to aim, but it was certainly capable of stopping a man in his tracks.

The principal weapon of the British soldier from 1902 was designated the Short, Magazine, Lee–Enfield rifle – SMLE to most soldiers. Based on its predecessor, now known as the 'long' Lee–Enfield, the intention was to build on the reliability of this arm (which had seen distinguished service in the Boer War), but to shorten it, lighten it, and provide the means of loading through a charger-fed magazine system. The resulting rifle, with it characteristic snubnose, was to appear on 23 December 1902 and undergo several modifications through to its last model, the Mark VI, in 1926. The SMLE Mark I was developed following experiences in the Boer War, which indicated that a lighter, more easily handled, better-sighting and quicker-loading weapon was needed. The charger system designed allowed for five rounds to be loaded at a time, the magazine holding ten all together. The early Mark I rifles had the provision for a long-range volley sight – inaccurate, but capable in the right hands of putting down a volley with an effective range of 1,500–2,000 yards.

Private Walter Astbury of the Cheshire Regiment, equipped with obsolete 1903 pattern bandolier equipment, and 'long' Lee–Enfield rifle. Private Astbury would depart for France in February 1915, and was to survive the war

Left: Pattern 1914 leather equipment set

Below: Soldier of the Royal East Kent Yeomanry, equipped with 1914 pattern leather equipment, and 'long' Lee–Enfield rifle

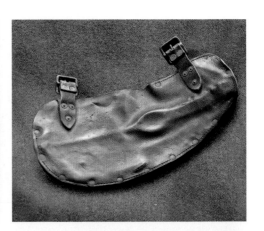

Clockwise from above: Entrenching tool helve and bayonet attachment used with the 1914 pattern set; cartridge carrier of the Pattern 1914 leather equipment; webbing haversack issued with the 1914 leather equipment set; well-used leather entrenching tool carrier; water bottle and cradle of the 1914 equipment set

Men of the Royal Garrison Artillery fully equipped with the 1903 bandolier equipment issued to mounted troops

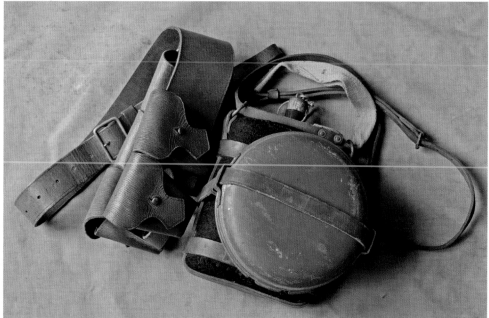

Bandolier, water bottle cradle and mess tin issued to mounted troops

Opposite: Soldier of the
4th Reserve Battalion
of the Buffs, equipped
with steel helmet, SMLE
rifle and Pattern 1914
leather equipment

Clockwise from right:
Officers in France, 1916;
officers' equipment, maps,
compass, notebooks, map
case; officers' equipment,
field glasses, vernier
compass and Very pistol

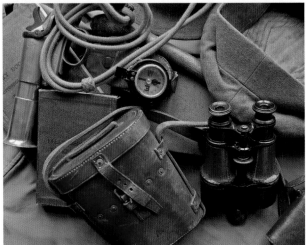

In wartime service was the SMLE Mark I***, introduced on 22 April 1914 in order to take the new Mark VII bullet, which required alteration to the sights. In addition, the SMLE Mark III, introduced in January 1907 with changes to its sights and charger loading system, was also to be used; from January 1916, simplifications to this rifle (SMLE Mark III*) were made in order to speed up production for the New Army. Amongst other things, the volley sights, no longer needed in trench warfare with the decline in musketry skills, were omitted.

With uniforms and equipment in short supply, it is not surprising that there was a poverty of weapons in the New Army. In August 1914, the whole stock of serviceable rifles stood just shy of 800,000, and just over half of these were the SMLE; with most of these weapons already issued, there was a reserve of no more than 10 per cent. With the two main manufacturers (the Royal Small Arms Factory, Enfield – RSA, and the Birmingham Small Arms Company – BSA) already committed, the War Office brought in two other companies to supply the SMLE (Vickers and the Standard Small Arms Company), and filled the gap with rifles from other countries. Ross rifles from Canada and Japanese Arisaka rifles were used in training by Kitchener's Army, alongside the obsolete 'long' Lee–Enfield; but none would be as admired as the SMLE.

With the development of a new, shorter SMLE rifle came the need for a longer bayonet; this was required as the likely enemy of the British soldier would be equipped with the longer Mauser-type rifle, meaning that Tommy would be at a disadvantage in a lunging bayonet fight. The original bayonet issued with the 'long' Lee–Enfield, the 1903 pattern, was only 12in long, and so inadequate to counter the threat of German blades if used with the SMLE. As such, the 1907 pattern

bayonet – always referred to as a 'sword' in British rifle regiments – was 5in longer than its predecessor; this would provide a reach comparable with any other existing weapons. The 1907 pattern bayonet attached to the SMLE by the use of a boss on the snub-nose of the SMLE (beneath the muzzle), and a bayonet bar, connecting with the mortise groove on the pommel of the bayonet. Early versions had hooked quillons; by 1914, this had been superseded by the simpler version with an uncomplicated crosspiece. Both versions had simple leather scabbards with steel top-mounts and tips (chapes) that were carried suspended from the belt by simple frogs.

Each soldier had to keep himself clean, tidy and presentable, even when in the trenches, and was issued with a set list of 'necessaries' under King's Regulations. Unless he was lucky enough to be a member of a rifle regiment – traditionally wearing black buttons and blackened insignia – brass fittings and insignia had to be burnished bright while out of the frontline, and uniforms kept clean and in good repair. In the frontline, of course, a more pragmatic approach had to be taken. It was expected that brasses should become dulled with exposure to the elements, as this would reduce the possibility of reflection off mirror-shined surfaces, and besides, the troops had more than enough to do keeping body and soul together. Nevertheless, soldiers were expected to attend to their own personal cleanliness as far as was possible, shaving regularly (often in the dregs of tea left in a tin cup or mess tin, the resulting suds tainting the next cup). This at least was an attempt to maintain morale.

Most of a soldier's necessaries were contained within a simple roll of cloth known as a 'holdall'. The holdall had a central strap of loops that were intended to hold a variety of objects of value in the everyday life of the soldier. Its purpose was to carry all those necessary items – and in accordance with clothing regulations, soldiers were expected to mark these small items of equipment using a punch for metal objects (or an engraving tool), or ink for cloth, with their regimental number (or the last four digits) and their regiment or corps. These items were: knife (often discarded), fork, spoon; cut-throat razor, shaving brush, toothbrush and comb; button stick; and sundry other items, such as bootlaces. For many young soldiers, shaving was a new experience, with downy cheeks requiring little more than a weekly shave. Army regulations required a clean chin, and although the pre-war army had expected that soldiers would maintain a moustache, in wartime the upper lip was also kept cleanly shaven. The standard issue was a Sheffield-produced cut-throat razor – usually with horn fittings upon which the soldier was expected to punch his regimental number and unit.

The holdall also had a convenient pocket that provided the means of holding additional items, including a shaving mirror – privately purchased – as well as soap, shaving requisites and the 'hussif' (housewife). The roll provided a practical means of keeping objects together – although for the frontline soldier, fork and spoon could conveniently be carried tucked into the puttees. The hussif was an essential piece of kit that held sewing materials: thread, needles, a thimble, wool, buttons and so on. The ravages of army life meant that some repair would be necessary, and so the housewife provided a method of keeping the uniform in at least some semblance of order; by 1917–18, with the proliferation of badges and patches, it also allowed the soldier to add insignia to his tunic. The hussif was simple in construction: a pocket of cotton material with a piece of serge for patching (and holding needles), closed by a flap.

Opposite: Clockwise from left: Rifles of the Durham Light Infantry; 'long' Lee–Enfield (far left) and the rest, SMLE; brass butt-plate of the SMLE (oil bottle and pull-through were stored in the butt); muzzle and fore-sight of the SMLE; the characteristic nose cap of the SMLE

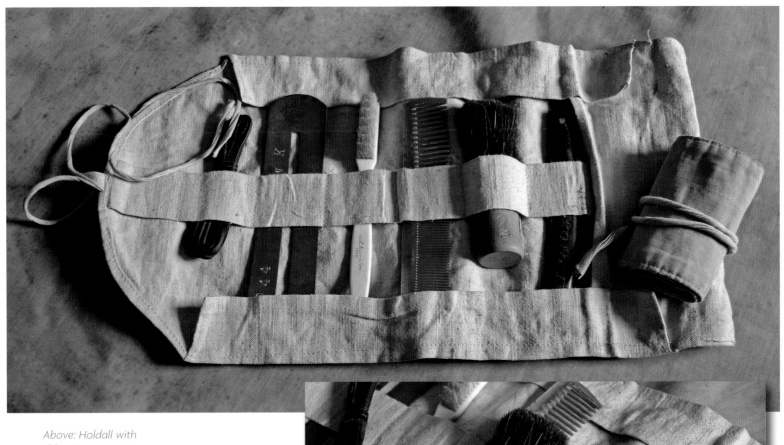

Above: Holdall with soldiers' 'necessaries'. Left to right: spare boot laces; button stick used to protect the uniform when polishing; toothbrush; comb; shaving brush and cut-throat razor. The small pouch is the 'housewife', the soldiers' sewing kit

Right: Cut-throat razor and shaving brush: soldiers' necessaries

IN TRAINING

The strains that had been felt by the army in supplying the influx of new men with uniforms and equipment were magnified when it came to housing the new recruits. With the Haldane reforms of the army in 1908 came a focus on a regimental depot located regionally in order to act as a centre for recruitment. Regiments that proudly carried the name of their county usually had a depot and barracks located within a prominent county town. It was from here that the two regular battalions found in most regiments served during peacetime, replacing each other overseas in turn in order to take on Imperial duties, garrisoning the outposts of Empire. Also in peacetime there was, in most cases, the third, Special Reserve, battalion, which acted as a 'home' to the recruits before they were posted to the regular battalions. These men would be housed in the regimental barracks, often located in old, purpose-built buildings, if austere, before going on to their regular postings.

For the part-time Territorials, 'home' would be one of the many drill halls scattered about the country, and it was here that soldiers would parade on Saturday afternoons – earning them the nickname 'Saturday night soldiers'. With the only obligation to house these men being an annual two-week camp for training, accommodation was usually less of an issue, and was typically in hutted or tented camps across Britain during the summer, when the weather was more forgiving to this type of accommodation. With the coming of war, and the creation of a mass citizen army, a major problem was the accommodation of large numbers of new recruits. Mass recruitment brought issues of space. Though in theory the first 100,000-strong tranche of Kitchener's New Army – K1 – could be housed in the regimental barracks vacated by those now serving overseas, the increasingly rapid flood of men who were joining the ranks in 1914–15 meant that new accommodation would be needed, and fast. Though some of the Pals' battalions raised by civic dignitaries would be housed in a diverse range of disused buildings – such as an old watch factory in Prescott for the Liverpool Pals – ultimately, there was a need to find new accommodation. The response was to build hutted encampments, but even these would require considerable investment of time. In the meantime, while the new camps were being built, tented accommodation was provided – adequate for a two-week Territorial field camp, but hardly the perfect setting to train an amateur army to the peak of military effectiveness. While some 800,000 men were accommodated in billets, the majority would be housed in tents while their huts were being built. With the weather worsening into the autumn of 1914, this was not an ideal situation, and muddy conditions made things unpleasant for many recruits – though later, tents were provided with wooden flooring.

Dear Sister
Just a few lines in answer to your PC which I got alright. We are up to the knees in mud and water it is not fit for pigs never mind men here. I expect to be home for Christmas.

Pte W. Astbury, 5th Battalion, Cheshire Regiment, Park Hall Camp, Oswestry

Above: Conditions in the barracks could be basic

Right: Barracks were often close to inhospitable for new recruits

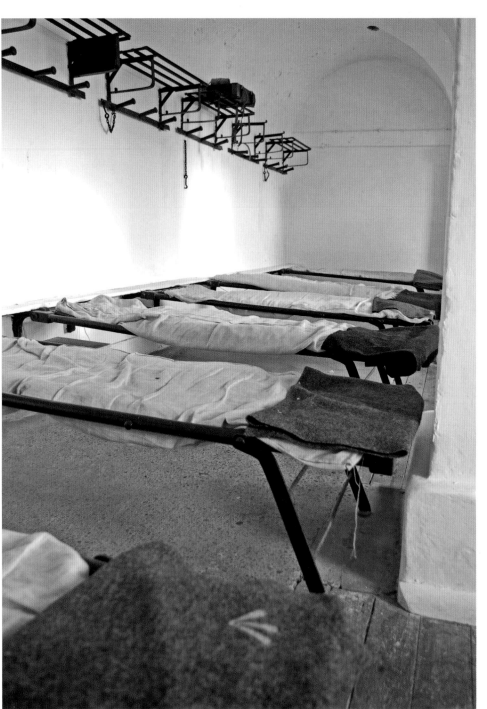

Large parts of rural Britain were given over to the new camps, particularly in the south, the historic geographical heart of the army. In the bell tents, men were expected to sleep in a radial pattern around the central pole. Those close to the entrance could find it unpleasant as men fumbled their way out to urinate at night, and the ground became increasingly muddy and unpleasant.

Dear Kitty
You will see by the address that we have shifted to another camp to make room for some new recruits, and the first night we got here we slept under canvas and it was raining and our beds were fairly floating in the morning so we had to shift from there.

Pte Percy Edwards, 3rd Battalion, South Wales Borderers, Moor Lane Camp, Nr Liverpool

By mid-1915, most of the tented accommodation had been replaced by wooden huts, and so conditions improved. Each camp developed its own character, and each one its routine. Postcards sent home from the camp set out to outline its regularity for the people back home:

The barracks of the Liverpool Pals, in a disused watch factory at Prescot, just outside the city

NO. P18   THE PALS' BARRACKS, PRESCOT.   Pub. by J. Edwa
Prescot

Above left: Aldershot and its surroundings were crowded with tented camps

Above right: Perham Down Camp, on the edge of Salisbury Plain, was replaced by huts in 1915

6.30	Reveille
6.45	Rouse Parade
7.00	Breakfast
8.15	Company Officer's Parade
8.45	Manoeuvres
11.15	Swedish Drill
1.00	Dinner
2.15	Rifle Drill
3.15	Lecture by Officer
4.30	Dismiss
5.00	Tea
6.00	Free Time
10.00	Last Post
10.15	Lights Out
10.30	Inspection of Guards

With accommodation basic in the extreme, it was the soldiers' canteens, and more specifically the 'dry' recreation huts provided by a large number of religious organisations, that were the social heart of the camps. The YMCA, the Church Army and the Salvation Army were the big providers, their huts paid for by charitable donations and 'flag days' – paper flags sold for coppers on the streets. These huts provided soft drinks, tea, sweets and the opportunity to write home on free notepaper – as well as providing billiard rooms and ping-pong – and were intended to persuade soldiers to spend more time engaging in wholesome pursuits, such as the game, House, rather than gambling or drinking. The Royal Army Temperance Association, set up in the nineteenth century, tried its hardest to get soldiers to sign its pledge 'watch and be sober', but with varying success.

With the men settled in their camps, the main job of the army instructors was to create a fit, efficient fighting force attuned to discipline and to be steady under fire, and they took their training seriously. As stated in *Infantry Training, 1914*: 'The object to be aimed at in the training of the infantry soldier

Soldiers of the Royal Army Medical Corps at a camp in southern England, c.1914

is to make him, mentally and physically, a better man than his adversary on the field of battle.' With large numbers of civilians coming into the army, training involved a simple diet of physical training, including the application of the Swedish drill system of 'physical jerks' – military-style gymnastics invented by Pehr Henrik Ling in the late nineteenth century – as well as long runs and the use of route marches in full equipment. With most men unused to such exercise, this was a new, challenging experience, one that was parodied mercilessly throughout the war.

Army Life in War Time

At doubling up and down the 'Square,' we've fairly learnt to do it,
The sergeant stands and shouts and swears, he fairly puts us thro' it;
Well then they give us Swedish Drill – so long it seems to last,
We often wish that we were 'Tanks,' and couldn't run so fast.

W.J. Stevenson

Soldiers of the Royal Field Artillery at a hutted camp, c.1914

It was the textbook *Infantry Training, 1914* that set out the training course syllabus: 1, the development of a soldierly spirit; 2, instruction in barrack and camp duties; 3, physical training; 4, infantry training; 5, marching and running; 6, musketry instruction; 7, movements at night; 8, guards and outposts; 9, duties of soldier in the field; 10, use of entrenching equipment; and 11, bayonet fighting. The average recruit might expect to receive training in all of these on his three-month journey to becoming a soldier.

Rather a trying day. Exceedingly hot. Busy at judging distances, fire control, and company drill, Swedish drill and semaphore. We dug 'trenches', supposedly under fire, lying face downwards and scratching out a shelter with our little entrenching tools – a frightful Sweat.

Pte D.H. Bell, London Rifle Brigade,
29 August 1914

Sketches of Tommy's life
In Training. — Nº 3
Getting your cup of tea in the morning was as exciting as a battle.

Competing for food was part of camp life

For the average soldier, military instruction included proper use of his principal weapon, the Short, Magazine, Lee–Enfield (SMLE) rifle, according to the *Musketry Regulations, Part 1* (1909, reprinted 1914): 'Musketry training is to render the individual soldier proficient in the use of small arms, to make him acquainted with the capabilities of the weapon with which he is armed, and to give him confidence in its power and accuracy.' But in Kitchener's New Army, valuable weapons such as the SMLE would be in short supply, and trainees would have to make do with wooden stand-ins or imports from Canada or Japan, while learning how to carry out manoeuvres with appropriate military bearing. The use of the bayonet was also deemed essential, and bayonet fighting would always be high on the training agenda.

The spirit of the bayonet is to be inculcated by describing the special feature of the bayonet and hand-to-hand fighting. The men must learn to practise bayonet fighting in the spirit and with the enthusiasm which animate them when training for their games …

Bayonet Training, 1916

Bayonet fighting in practice would be no game. Such training, as described by Rifleman Groom of the London Rifle Brigade, involved charging sacks marked with discs denoting head, eyes and heart, yelling like maniacs as they struck home. Details of bayonet training were often graphic; many found the experience terrifying.

Clockwise from below: Field kitchen cookers at a camp; tools of the cooks' trade; cooks prepare a meal; dishing out food to recruits at a camp in England

*Enjoying a meal at
a hutted camp near
Wareham. Frank Ward,
second man from the left
on the front bench, would
be killed in Flanders*

Right: Inside a Church Army hut. Such huts were the social hub of camps at home and in France

Below: YMCA huts provided simple refreshment, games and a chance to write home

Recruits engage in 'physical jerks' and Swedish drill, c.1914. A frame for bayonet practice is visible behind them

Clockwise from right: Bed rolls had to be stored during the day at barracks across the country; kit inspection was a feature of barrack life, here laid out by a private in the Devonshire Regiment; artillery men were equipped with 1903 Bandolier equipment

Opposite: Kit layout for an infantryman in the Devonshire Regiment. Boots, rifle, equipment, uniform and necessaries had to be in good order

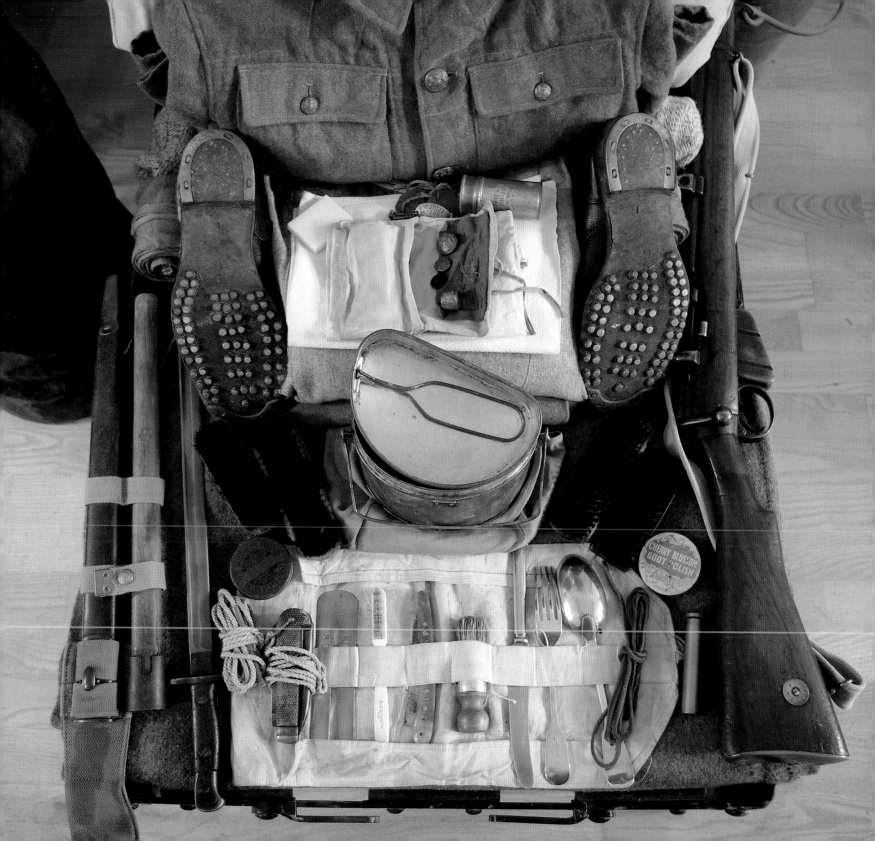

Sketches
of Tommy's life

In Training. — N° 8

You are a Trained Soldier as soon as you finish your firing course. It's hard to shoot well at this time, on account of having so many to help you hit the bulls eye.

Musketry practice was an essential part of recruit training

Dear Kitty
Well I have settled down to my new life alright because its no use breaking your heart here, just as that song says pack up your troubles in your old kit bag and smile. You should have seen us today on bayonet fighting we were half mad the man who can pull the ugliest face and do the most shouting is the best.

Pte Percy Edwards, 3rd Battalion, South Wales Borderers, Sniggery Camp, Nr Liverpool

For later war recruits, such as Private Hodges of the Bedfordshire Regiment, weapons use was a significant component of the training, including the correct deployment of the Mills grenade – a function of the needs of trench warfare.

For all, training on the rifle range was the opportunity to fire live rounds. Officers too would be expected to gain proficiency. At late stages of the war, training also involved acclimatisation to gas warfare – the correct fitting of the respirator and the entry into gas chambers intended to check both the nerves of the wearer and the adequacy of the equipment. Specialist training – for the coveted scout, signaller or expert marksman's badges, for example – would also be offered for those of ability. In return, as well as the badges, extra pay would be forthcoming. Variable in length, the average recruit would receive at least three months of training at home before often being inspected by a general, Kitchener, or the king himself, and proceeding overseas.

Dear Sister
The King came to review us today and I can tell you it was a sight. We then all marched past him and then we formed a guard of honour to the station. It was a sight I shall never forget. I expect we go on Saturday, the King told our Colonel. Your Loving Brother Walter

Pte W. Astbury, 5th Battalion, Cheshire Regiment, Cambridge

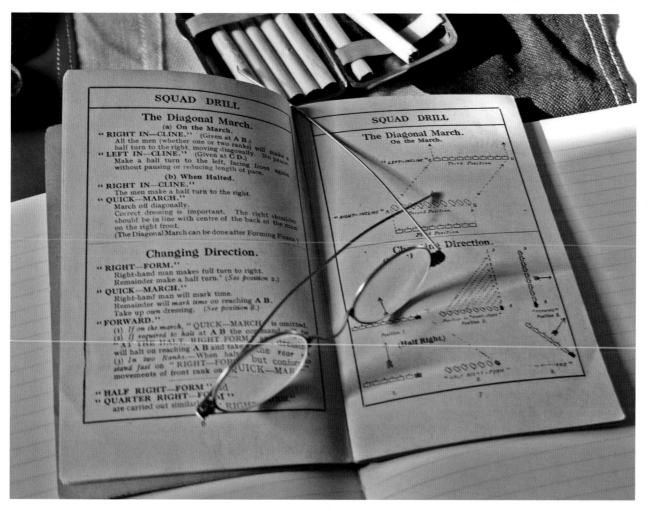

Drill and training were set out in a series of army texts

FORT MATILDA
GREENOCK
9 NOV 14
My dear Suffield,
thank you very much
indeed for your share of the flask, a

UP THE LINE

I daresay you are anxious to know how I got on if I arrived safe I did quite safely. I arrived at the rest Camp Somewhere in France about 9 on Wednesday night. We have got to the place where we have got to do some more training … The French people gave us a good greeting as went through 2 of their big towns but I don't care for their streets and houses are too dirty for my liking. I rather enjoyed my ride across.

Pte James Moore, Nottinghamshire and Derbyshire Regiment

GOING OVERSEAS

With the great mass of recruits joining in 1914–15, there was a fear amongst some that they would not even get as far as France and Flanders before the war had ended. This feeling was natural, especially so since the regulars had already left for the front and the newspapers were full of stories of gallant Tommies 'at the front', taking their part in the 'great game'.

In your letter you mention about the war … overhearing one of the Aldershot knuts & it being over by March, I don't think. My idea is that it will last a bit longer than that, also you don't expect anything exciting yet a while, well every man cannot play International for England against Germany, but you never know you might be one of the selected.

Letter to Pte Harry Flewitt, 12th Battalion, King's Liverpool Regiment, 9 December 1914

Starting from an initial number of just six regular divisions (1st–6th), the War Office assembled a further fifty-nine divisions: six Regular, thirty New Army,

Opposite: Lieutenant Christopher Wilkinson Brown, Royal Scots Fusiliers, describes training in 1914

Left: The journey to the front commenced at railway stations up and down Britain

Opposite Page:
Left: Divisional signs:
38th (Welsh) Division
(dragon); 40th Division
(cock); 37th Division
(horseshoe); 16th (Irish)
Division (shamrock);
19th (Western) Division
(butterfly); 30th Division
(eagle and child);
55th (West Lancashire)
Division (red rose)

Right: Battalion
and divisional signs,
1/1st Battalion
Hertfordshire Regiment,
37th Division

fifteen First Line Territorial (composed of soldiers who had signed the Imperial Service Obligation in the first instance), fourteen Second Line Territorial, a Yeomanry division, three Home Service Division and one compiled from Royal Naval Reservists – the Royal Naval Division. Of this total of seventy-five available divisions, sixty-five would actually see action overseas.

Each division was made up of almost 20,000 men, with the infantry forming the greatest number: comprising, in the early part of the war, some 12,000 men divided between three infantry brigades, in turn composed of three infantry battalions each. In addition, an infantry battalion was attached to the division that was designated as 'Divisional Pioneers' – soldiers who would, as well as carrying a rifle, have to wield pick and shovel. The remainder was composed of the fighting arms, such as the Artillery and Engineers (making up some 5,000 men), and the Services, such as the Army Service Corps, which was required to supply the needs of the division in the field, and the cavalry.

The first six divisions had landed in France by mid-September 1914 – though the first four landed there on 17 August – a triumph of preparation and organisation. The remainder of the regular divisions had crossed to France by January 1915 (though the last to be formed, the 29th Division, was sent to Gallipoli). The first of the First Line Territorials followed in February 1915, though eight of these were sent to other theatres, such as Egypt, Palestine or Gallipoli: most were in the field by August 1915. For the New Army men, training and assembly meant that they would have to wait some months before they could be committed to action. The first New Army divisions to go were the 9th (Scottish) and 14th (Light) Divisions, arriving in France and Flanders in May 1915; with four

divisions committed to other theatres (Gallipoli and Egypt), the remainder would transfer to France in the latter part of 1915 and into the spring of 1916 – ready to be committed to the coming offensive on the Somme, in July 1916. The last divisions to go were the Second Line Territorials, formed originally from men who had signed on only for Home Service, but who, with the advent of the Military Service Act in 1916, were compelled to fight abroad from May 1916.

With so many units in the field by 1916–17, an effective system of identifying units as components of a larger formation was needed, to be used widely on the transport, in the headquarters and on the men themselves. Left largely to the whim of the commanders of these units, a series of identifying badges was developed that could be painted on battalion transports and the like. Often colourful, these generally referred to the regional origin of the formation, like the thistle of the 9th (Scottish) Division, the red dragon of the 38th (Welsh) Division or the red rose of the 55th (West Lancashire) Division. Or they used a symbol that indicated the number or origin of the division – like the bantam cock of the 40th Division, modified with the addition of an acorn to commemorate the capture of Bourlon Wood on the Somme in 1916, or the broken spur of the 74th Division, composed largely of dismounted Yeomanry troops. Others would be more obscure; the dot and dash of the 17th Division (representing the top of the number 17), for example. Late war, cloth versions of these devices would be sewn to the upper sleeve of the Service Dress, and an even more complex system of brigade and battalion cloth signs would find its way onto the uniform sleeve, or even the back of the soldier, just below his collar.

Preparation to go overseas required the completion of training, and the required course of musketry, using both the SMLE and a smaller-bore .22 rifle for target shooting. Yet Skill at Arms training would not necessarily translate into action in the field. Inoculations were essential, with soldiers being vaccinated for smallpox, tetanus and typhoid; the act was feared, with many soldiers suffering from fevers in the wake of the treatment.

Vaccinated today; the Medical Officer did 10 men in an hour, which is pretty smart work. We filed bare-armed past him, were scratched with a nasty little implement, and the lymph was applied.

Pte D.H. Bell, London Rifle Brigade

A man went overseas as a member of his battalion (or, as time passed in this long war, as a replacement to make up the losses sustained through casualties). Leave was granted before proceeding overseas; all too short, parting at rail termini was heart wrenching for many. With the stations packed with soldiers,

tearful relatives, regimental bands and NCOs barking orders, the emotionally charged atmosphere had a sincere effect on many soldiers.

A draft went off at 6.15 on Sunday morning: the Tommies were singing their extraordinary and unique songs as usual. A lot of men were from my company & they said they would see me alright in Berlin – they think they are in for a bean feast. As the train leaves with a draft the pipers always play the regimental tune 'Hieland Laddie' and it seemed very weird at that dark & early hour, lots of fellows will have heard that for the last time.

2nd Lt Christopher Wilkinson Brown, 3rd Battalion Royal Scots Fusiliers, Fort Matilda, Greenock, 9 November 1914

To the regular soldiers of the BEF in August 1914, Lord Kitchener would give a personal message: a slip of paper that was to be treated as 'confidential', and carried in their pay book.

You are ordered abroad as a soldier of the King to help our French comrades against the invasion of a common enemy … Remember that the honour of the British Army depends on your individual conduct.

ON THE BULL RING.

The 'Bull Ring'; the training ground of the major base camps in France

Sketches
of Tommy's life
At the Base. — Nº 6

But we also tried hard to kill ourselves, before we could gep up the Line, by
tearing like mad up and down a lot of sand hills in full fighting order

*Training on 'the Pimple'
at Le Havre*

It will be your duty not only to set an example of discipline and perfect steadiness under fire but also to maintain the most friendly relations with those whom you are helping in this struggle … In this new experience you may find temptations both in wine and women. You must entirely resist both …

Kitchener, Field Marshal, August 1914

Draughts were invariably to leave the country through Dover or later Folkestone if their destination was France; Southampton if elsewhere.

Dearest Kitty.
Just a brief note to let you know that I am in the pink hoping you are the same. I had a very pleasant crossing across the water. I suppose Gerty drives you mad now that I am across the water and Jack in Blighty. I think it will be a long while before we meet again but I hope it will come very soon.

Pte Percy Edwards, 3rd Battalion,
South Wales Borderers

Above: RAMC football team, 2nd Division

Right: Training medals awarded at the base camps of the British Expeditionary Force in France

The destination of the cross-Channel troop ships was Boulogne, Calais, Rouen or Le Havre; for most, arrival at their destination would involve a further period of training – battle hardening and acclimatisation to local conditions that saw, in France at least, the use of vast base camps (known as 'infantry base depots') and harsh training in so-called 'bull rings', such as those at Etaples ('heel taps' or 'eat apples' to Tommy) and Le Havre.

Evening found us at the great base camp at Etaples in a vast wilderness of tents and buildings. For mile on mile the camp stretched along the dunes. I was awed at the vast array which spoke of the growing might of the British Expeditionary Force.

Lt Charles Douie, 1st Battalion, Dorsetshire Regiment

The most infamous of the bull rings was that at Etaples; a vast area in the dune fields that was presided over by 'canaries': physical training instructors distinguished by their yellow armbands and the crossed swords of the drill instructor. At Le Havre, a hill known as 'the Pimple' was to feature prominently in the soldiers' physical training.

Thirty thousand men learnt the advanced lessons of war on the 'Pimple.' They bayoneted, manoeuvred and trained from seven in the morning until four in the afternoon … They listened to the most bloodthirsty lectures ever conceived, from the lips of hard-bitten instructors who had seen everything since Mons.

Pte Arthur E. Lambert, 2nd Battalion, HAC

Team games such as football – and sport in general – were also a feature of life at the base camps. As the war lasted longer than anyone expected, the British Expeditionary Force instigated cups and medals as an incentive to soldiers to try their best. Certainly, this was good for the morale of the average sport-loving soldier.

Overseas, further equipment issues were required to help support the soldier in the frontline. The first of these was identification discs. Identity discs have not always been part of the soldier's traditional accoutrements in the British Army; identity was originally provided by the Soldier's Service and Pay Book (Army Form AB64), which was carried in the right breast pocket of the Service Dress. Now inadequate, this form of identification was supplemented by a single stamped aluminium disc, which carried name, rank, serial number, unit details and religion (where appropriate), and which was issued on mobilisation in 1914, later issues being a single red fibre disc. Although the disc was hardier than the pay book, there was, nonetheless, a problem: once this single disc was removed from the body, as stipulated in *Field Service Regulations*, the chances of identification were much reduced.

As such, in August 1916, a two-disc system was developed, the discs themselves carrying the same information before, in duplicate, but this time stamped on compressed vulcanised asbestos discs: a green octagonal one, which, it was intended, would stay with the body; and a red disc, which would be taken as part of the accounting procedure. Both were to be worn on a string around the neck, but, as this often became dirty and clammy, soldiers were wont to carry the discs separately in the haversack or pack, or to rely on the commercially available metal versions that were produced at home and abroad. All were to

Identity discs as issued to Private Bill Pratt (left); and locally made identity bracelets as often worn by soldiers (right)

be given the brutally frank name 'cold meat tickets' (resembling as they did the tags used in butchers' shops), as the war dragged on. As was typical, local entrepreneurs soon adapted their trade to produce engraved or stamped versions for the troops in rear areas and base camps.

Field dressings were issued to all soldiers, to be kept in a pocket under the front flap of the Service Dress tunic. This was intended for rudimentary first aid, and consisted of a packet containing two dressings: one for the entry wound, one for the exit (in the case of gunshot wounds). Early on, these pouches also contained safety pins and ampoules of

iodine as a form of disinfectant to treat the wound; later in the war, the value of the chemical having been questioned, it was left out of the set. In all cases, the idea was that a wounded man would have his own dressings used upon him. With so many wounds being caused by shell fire, however, larger dressings were needed than could be carried by an individual, and these special 'shell dressings' were carried by regimental stretcher-bearers in action.

In preparation for their first tour of the trenches, soldiers were also invited to make out their wills. This was completed in the official record of their military service, the pay book. It was on page 13 of the AB64 that the pro forma will was provided; soldiers moving up the line for the first time were to complete this – an act that was seen to be tempting fate by many. The pay book served as a logbook of service, but also included personal and family details (including next of kin), regimental number, dates of enlistment, ranks and awards attained, skill at arms, charges, a sick record, and a record of pay issued. Pre-war, the soldier was issued with a linen-covered Small Book; this was to be replaced with the issue of AB64, Soldier's Service and Pay Book, to every soldier on enlistment. This acted as a passport; a document that was to be carried at all times and to be produced on request for examination by officers or regimental/military police. The AB64 was a valuable document, proof of identification both as a battlefield casualty and when receiving pay.

Essential for all soldiers going up the line was the issue of 'iron rations' – food to be carried in action, intended to provide sustenance only under the direst circumstances. Iron rations comprised a can of bully beef, some biscuits, and a tin containing tea and sugar. It was a 'crime' to dip into these rations unless the order was given to do so from an officer, and they were to be used only in an emergency. Carried in the haversack, or sometimes in a small cloth bag (intended for the 'unexpired' portion of a day's ration) attached to the belt or equipment, these rations would be carried into action, along with a full water bottle. Bully beef was so prevalent in the trenches that most soldiers tired of it; for Private Hodges of the Bedfordshire Regiment, Fray Bentos was the preferred brand. The accompanying army biscuits were so hard that men had to have reasonable teeth – a requirement of the medical inspection on enlistment – to bite into

First Field Dressing, issued 1918

them, or they had to be ground into a powder and mixed with water to make rudimentary desserts or to bulk up food in the frontline.

Tommy began his journey from the base camps to the frontline in notoriously slow-moving trains, housed in trucks marked '*Hommes 8, Chevaux 40*' (which led to some speculation if this was either/or, or if the horses were to join the forty men in the truck). Travelling at speeds that approached walking pace, the journey was long, drawn out and frustrating. At the very least, it was a relief to know that, finally, he was to go 'up the line'. With frequent halts along the way, soldiers would walk up to the engine in order to beg water for tea, and as the trains passed through the countryside, making stops at rural stations, they were invariably pursued by children begging for trinkets, souvenirs and food.

'Bulle-e, biscuits – Tomm-e-ee!' That shrill piping cry yelled by the horde of squawking, squalid and jostling children scrambling about on the station siding greeted me as I stepped out of the crowded homes [sic] et chevaux truck and left the slow, dirty troop train with a sigh of utter relief.

Rifleman Giles Eyre, King's Royal Rifle Corps

With the French rail system tightly controlled, clogged with troops and materiel bound for the front, these journeys were laborious, but would end at a railhead in Belgium or northern France. From these dispersal points, movement to the front was mostly by foot. The going was hard, particularly upon the *pavé* roads typical of this corner of Europe, composed of tough cobblestones smoothed by constant traffic. With soldiers' boots heavily cleated it was difficult to maintain balance, and the unyielding stone would jar the body every time a heavy boot was put upon the ground. A soldier's equipment came to hang heavy on his shoulders.

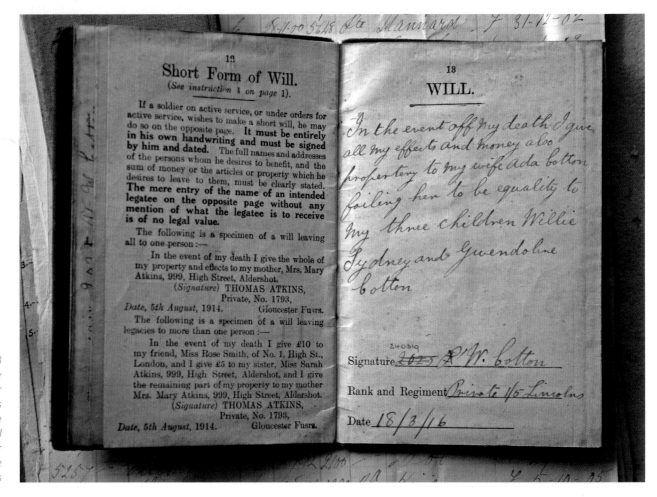

Will made out on page 18 of the Service and Pay Book. Private Walter Cotton leaves all his effects to his wife. Private Cotton was invalided out of the army after being downgraded to the Labour Corps

Iron rations

For hour upon hour … the long column moved forward. In fifty-minute stretches it trudged up hill and down dale and never were minutes so leaden. Sixty pounds needs lifting at all, but to carry it upon one's shoulders for successive hours is almost indescribable. The leather straps cut into the shoulders, the pack brings on an intolerable backache that never really disappears, the haversack on one side and the water bottle on the other, rub the skin from the thighs, and the rifle gets weightier every mile.

Pte Arthur E. Lambert, 2nd Battalion,
Honourable Artillery Company

For some luckier soldiers, transport to the front might, incongruously, be by London omnibus, suitably painted and boarded for frontline use. Though soldiers often complained that they never saw an omnibus in France, by the end of the war there were as many as 650 vehicles operating to deliver men forward – with a capacity for 13,300 men – their crews living, sleeping and eating in their vehicles. The badge of the 16th Auxiliary Omnibus Company, Army Service Corps – Britannia (from the penny coin) – harked back to happier days, with its motto, 'Penny all the Way'. For the final part of their journey, all soldiers would be marched in, up the line, the booming of the guns an ominous sign of their arrival in the danger zone.

Here we turned off to the right and left the pavé road which runs on to Ypres, and after this the roads were much more difficult to travel. Shell holes were frequent and generally full of water, so that in the dark it was only too easy to stumble into them. 'Shell-hole on the right,' 'Shell-hole on the left,' 'Shell-hole in the middle,' 'Keep to your right' were being passed back continually. Progress was slow of course under these conditions and with the heavy loads that we all carried. But

Soldiers in France were often plagued by hordes of children looking for food or souvenirs

BOO-LEE BEE-E-E-F ?
BIS-KWEET ?

HOMMES 40
CHEVAUX 8

F. Mackain

Sketches
of Tommy's life
At the Base. — Nº 8

We left the Base in great style and in cattle trucks. We must have averaged a good mile an hour. The juvenile population along the way make earnest enquiries concerning our « iron rations ».

An ASC driver. If they were lucky, soldiers got transport to the front; most often they marched

it was all so novel to me that I had not a moment to feel dull or depressed. After a time we reached the notorious 'Shrapnel Corner' and turned towards 'Transport Farm', for we were bound for trenches at Hill 60.

Capt. Francis Buckley, 7th Battalion,
Northumberland Fusiliers

UP THE LINE

'Up the line': to the unseasoned volunteer and conscript, this phrase signified that, for them at least, the war had definitely arrived. To those new to the front, the first taste of trench duty would be a defining moment in their military careers, if not their lives. Issued with iron rations and a full complement of 250 rounds of ammunition (150 in pouches, 100 in two cotton bandoliers), it was an ominous sign that soldiers were instructed to destroy any personal papers that could identify them, and to fill in the personal will section of their pay books. At this point, letters would be hurriedly written – 'in the pink' – and the men would move up the line via duckboards and communication trenches (CTs), to replace soldiers only too happy to leave. Trench stores would be handed over from one battalion to another, and the officers would set to work ensuring that sentries were deployed and the nocturnal life of the trenches could begin. For most soldiers, to have served up the line had a special cachet: the 'wounded' or wound stripe (a gold stripe to be worn on the uniform, and awarded for every occasion of wounding); the authentic wear-and-tear on the uniform, mud on the boots. These would all mark out the soldier who had done his tour, typically five to seven days in the frontline trenches, before going out in reserve and, finally, on-rest. Rest, anathema to the army, meant training by day and, by night, up the line again on fatigue parties.

The march into the trenches

Trench warfare has assumed an almost mythical status today, the phrase 'in the trenches' being almost synonymous with service in the First World War. For most British soldiers, trench warfare was to be the norm, even in far-flung theatres such as Gallipoli and Salonika. Derided by the army High Command as a 'phase of warfare' that would soon be transformed into open warfare, 'the trenches' would exist from their first

Sketches of Tommy's life **Up the line – N° 3**

We marched into the Trenches, late in the evening, going across fields on « duck boards ». There is nothing to be seen but shell-holes, and wintry looking trees.

inception in September 1914 through to the opening of the Battle of Amiens in August 1918, and the final Advance to Victory.

The Western Front became an entity once the opposing forces had entrenched across northern Europe, in late 1914, and it was on the Western Front that trenches became the dominant feature of warfare. Trenches varied according to use, and their construction became more sophisticated as the war dragged on. In Flanders, the construction of trenches was mostly a battle with the prevailing geological conditions, as the combination of water-repelling clay and overlying water-retaining sands meant that, when it rained, the heavily shelled ground became the muddy quagmire we associate with the Great War. Elsewhere, such as on the Somme, trenches could be founded in startlingly white chalks, overlain by sticky clays and silts, which would dry to a choking dust in summer, and be churned to a cloying mud in the winter.

The simple purpose of the trenches was, of course, to provide protection to the frontline troops and their supporting arms in the face of small arms fire (rifles, machine guns and the like) and artillery. Once the trench lines reached practically unbroken from the sea to the fortress of Belfort on the Swiss border, outflanking movements were no longer an option, and the stalemate of the trenches became the norm for four long years of war. In their simplest sense, trenches were linear excavations of variable depth that were mostly open to the sky, but were sometimes roofed for concealment purposes, usually with close-boarded timber – but this was rare. For the most part, they were between 6ft and 8ft deep, with a prescribed depth, according to High Command, of 5ft 9in in dry soil, with a further 9in of soil built up as a parapet. This, of course, was the ideal, for in some cases it was impossible to dig more than a foot or so before reaching water-saturated ground, especially

in the Ypres Salient, with its underlying foundation of water-repelling clay. Here, instead, the trenches were built up rather than dug down, creating what was known as 'High Command' or 'Parapet' trenches. Walls were usually of the ubiquitous sandbags filled with whatever was closest to hand – but preferably sandy soils capable of stopping the rounds that buzzed across no man's land. In other situations, boxes or gabions were used as the basis for the parapet. In order to achieve this, specially constructed, inverted 'A' frames were used in order to support both the sloping walls of the trenches and the duckboard flooring.

Trenches were laid out by the Royal Engineers – that most versatile of the corps of the Royal Engineers – but were dug by the infantry. In fact, some sixty-eight infantry battalions would be transformed into Pioneers, and each division received one of these newly designated units. Men of the Pioneer Battalions – distinguished by their crossed rifle and pick collar badges – were equipped and trained as fighting soldiers, but were skilled enough to provide essential labour building roads, digging dugouts and maintaining services. Later in the war, medically downgraded men – often men recovered from wounds or illness – would be transferred into the Labour Corps to provide essential labour in the rear areas. They too would be called upon to fight in an emergency.

Yet no infantryman could escape digging. All were equipped with a clever personal entrenching tool, which comprised a steel head of combined spade and pick, and a separate wooden handle called a helve. These tools were supplied to provide a means of digging a shallow scrape in an emergency, or for a multitude of other small jobs in the field, acting as hammer, pick and digging tool. It is doubtful that entrenching tools were used to dig many trenches; for that the ubiquitous General Service (GS) spades were

Above: Royal Engineers equipped with General Service (GS) spades

Right: The General Service pick and spade

needed. These spades were issued to the battalion at the rate of 110 per battalion: open-mouthed, with a turned-back top to protect the spade from the heavy boot of the infantryman, they were used in earnest in the digging of frontline trenches. The time estimated in 1914 (as prescribed by the officer's *Field Service Pocket Book*) for digging a man's length of fire trench – two paces, or 45 cubic feet – was 100 minutes under normal conditions. Heavy picks were also provided,

with seventy-six issued per battalion, and were there to break the ground so the spademen could then do their work. Both tools would be used in digging trenches throughout the war and, under the orders of sapper officers and NCOs, the infantry would provide the manpower to do so. Spades and picks were often carried into action by infantrymen and, famously, by the leading assault troops on the Somme in 1916. This was to allow for the turning of trench lines once

Working parties would have to carry up a number of trench structures, including duckboards, designed to fit one into another

I' ve got a cushy job now !

captured, with the reversal of the fire-step from one side to the other.

Most trenches were 'floored' with wooden duck-boards, which were built up to allow drainage beneath – in fact it was common for successive levels of duck-boards to be laid one on top of another to combat the difficult conditions encountered. In rare cases, bricks and rubble were used when trench lines snaked through the destroyed villages and houses.

We are in a real trench this time, one of the few, I suppose, which survived the wet weather. It's really very luxurious, for the bottom is all paved with brick or boarded over; and though naturally there is still a deal of mud in places, we are quite happy.

Lt A.D. Gillespie, Argyll and Sutherland Highlanders, March 1915

Ensuring the trench was adequately drained and floored was essential if the men were not to suffer from the elements as well as the constant shellfire.

The sticky mud yoicked one's boots off nearly, and it felt as if one's foot would be broken in extricating it. We all wore gum-boots, of blue-black rubber, that come right up to the waist like fishermen's waders. But the mud is everywhere, and we get our arms all plastered with it as we literally 'reel to and fro' along the trench, every now and again steadying ourselves against slimy sand-bags. One or two men actually got stuck, and had to be helped out with spades.

Lt B. Adams, Royal Welsh Fusiliers, 1915

Trench sides (known as slopes) were supported or 'revet-ted' with whatever was available, sometimes wattle, often corrugated sheeting and expanded metal (xpm), sometimes chicken wire, or even timber boards if available. Timber was universally used to hold these materials in place, and layers of bonded sandbags strengthened the whole. Recent archaeology in Flanders has uncovered the remains of these *in situ*, and has supported the notion of a constant battle between man and nature in keeping the trenches in some kind of order – essential for the maintenance of morale.

A Company had two platoons in the front line trench 41, some 100 yards from the enemy, and two platoons in a support line called '41 support'. The trenches themselves were well-built and revetted with sand bags, and dry enough even during the wettest weather. We had in these days only small shelters – the deep dugout was unknown.

Capt. Francis Buckley, 7th Battalion, Northumberland Fusiliers

The function of trenches varied, though in the main there were two consistent types: fire trenches, which formed the frontline; and communication trenches, which joined them. Fire trenches (i.e. fighting trenches) were divided into a regular pattern of fire bays and traverses, which meant that no soldier could walk in a straight line for long without having to switch back on himself. This was intended to limit the effects of shellfire, or the possibility of rifle and machine-gun fire along the length of a trench – with inevitable consequences. British and German fire trenches were alike in this respect; French versions often had a more leisurely, curved, sinuous line. The spoil removed in digging a trench was used to form a *parapet* – a mound of earth in front of the trench on the enemy side – and a *parados* – a slightly higher mound at the rear. In areas where groundwater was close to the surface, 'borrow pits' were dug on either side of the trench to supply extra earth needed to build up a sufficient height to protect the troops. Each fire trench was equipped with a fire-step, ideally of regulation 2ft high and 18in wide, sufficient to raise an average man's head above the protection of the parapet, when required to do so.

Fire trenches were usually arranged in successive parallel rows, with the frontline, support line and reserve line all connected by the communication trenches, which were the main thoroughfares of trench warfare. In well-established trench systems the frontline consisted of a fire trench and ancillary support trench with deeper dugouts providing accommodation for the troops. This system was achieved in the mid part of the war; by its end, more flexible systems, involving forward outposts, were in place. Throughout the war, dugouts were to evolve from simple scrapes in the trench slopes – providing

Clockwise from above: Trenches were intentionally formed of bays and traverses to reduce the lateral extent of artillery or gunfire; trench boards gave direction in the trenches themselves; mid-war, trench revetments were held in place with wire-anchored angle-iron stakes

little more than limited cover and often requiring the occupant to stretch his legs out into the main trench line – to deeper affairs dug or 'mined' to provide protection from the attentions of howitzer shells and trench mortars. In most cases, accommodation in the trenches was squalid.

It is up to eyes in mud out here, I don't know what you would say if you could see me now sat in a hole in the railway bank with a couple of old sheets of corrugated iron over it to keep the rain off, and my clothes covered in mud. But we have got a fire so we think ourselves lucky.

Pte Herbert Dando, 1st Battalion, The Queen's (Royal West Surrey Regiment)

Due to the complexities of the growing trench systems, it was possible to get hopelessly lost, and so trench signboards were fixed to allow newcomers to a particular stretch to get orientated. Trenches were named or numbered, according to the preference of the commanders in charge, and were often themed: matching initial letters, the names of towns or villages, or common city streets being typical. In most cases, it was necessary to direct soldiers through the maze of trenches, for although they were theoretically constructed in parallel lines – at least in the early stages of trench warfare on the Western Front – the re-entrants, salients and redoubts would be interconnected by communication trenches (CTs) and minor trenches intended as latrines, entrances to dugouts, trench mortar batteries, and so on. This created a confusing mess of ditches.

There was one junction of trenches where one had to cross a dyke full of half-frozen water; there was always congestion of troops here, ration parties, relieving parties, and ourselves.

Lt B. Adams, Royal Welsh Fusiliers, 1915

With men stumbling along the lines, often under the cover of darkness, it was all too easy to take a wrong turn. And for those relieving battalions, taking over positions from those at the front, it was doubly confusing. Guides would often have to be appointed to assist them.

Most soldiers would travel to the frontline from the rear areas along crowded CTs at night – bustling, narrow thoroughfares 6ft deep with barely enough room for men to pass. Although relieving battalions would be guided to the front by experienced soldiers from the battalion about to be relieved, to direct them, sign boards would still be necessary, picked out by candlelight. Like the frontline, many of the long CTs had picturesque names, chosen at will and whim, which were painted on rough and crude boards. Such boards would also exist in the frontline; and others, with a more urgent message, might warn of the dangers from snipers, artillery fire or the physical hazards of loose or low wires, or treacherous duckboards.

This complex system grew throughout the war, and was recorded on equally complex trench maps. The purpose of communication trenches was to link the forward or fire trenches, and to allow men, munitions and supplies to travel up to the line – as well as wounded soldiers to come out of the line. For this reason, they were wide enough to allow stretcher-bearers to carry out their duties. Very often these trenches bore names such as 'alley', 'lane' or 'street', indicating their intended purpose. Running from the rear

Sketches
of Tommy's life

Up the line — N° 10

Sometimes you get so far in the rear, marching in, you are as good as lost
when you come to a spot where different trenches branch off.

*Finding direction in the
maze of trench lines was
often challenging*

areas and connecting all the forward trenches up to the frontline, they offered protection for supply and troop movements from the rear. They were usually dug in a zigzag or wavy pattern and in Flanders, where the geological conditions meant that revetment was essential, they had similar dimensions to a fire trench. In some cases (such as at Arras, and Nieuport on the Belgian coast), CTs were replaced by underground subways, which provided much more protection from the searching enemy artillery.

Between the frontlines of the opposing trenches was no man's land, a strip of contested ground that varied in width from a few feet to tens of yards. The term was coined early in the war, but already had a long history as the name for a forbidding place. It was certainly that: the dead ground between the opposing trenches that was bordered by dense thickets of barbed wire – an unwelcoming place, particularly if the ground had been silent witness to a raid or attack 'over the bags'.

*Another feature of the place was the awful nature
of the ground outside the trenches. It was a morass
filled with partially buried bodies – that is,
partially buried by nature in the ooze and mud.*

During a dense mist about seventy identity discs were recovered from the ground behind our support lines. And it was worse in front between the opposing trenches.

Capt. Francis Buckley, 7th Battalion, Northumberland Fusiliers

Tactical possession of no man's land was claimed by many, with aggressive patrolling, raids and observation being the common practice of British battalions. But it was also more often than not a dumping ground for waste materials; in some cases, soldiers were encouraged to fling tins and food containers over the parapet. Though there were obvious concerns over the hygiene of this practice, in many ways it made sense: snipers could hide behind such debris, while would-be attackers might stumble over the waste tins and create a racket, alerting the sentry. It was not to all officers' tastes, however.

I gaze across into No Man's Land. I can just see our wire, and in front a collection of old tins — bully tins, jam tins, butter tins — paper, old bits of equipment. Other regiments always leave places so untidy.

Lt B. Adams, Royal Welsh Fusiliers, 1915

No man's land was crossed when soldiers went over the top; when they climbed out over the parapet to face the enemy. For the most part, this ground was observed by day through trench periscopes set up for the purpose; putting one's head above the trench was virtually suicidal, and head injuries were common in tall soldiers and the curious, especially so before the advent of the steel helmet in 1915–16. By night, sentries were expected to look out over the ground in front of the parapet — a dangerous business when the machine guns were trained at head height to counter this eventuality, and when trenches might only be yards apart.

Trench sign for 'Stout Track' from south of the Menin road, in the Ypres Salient. It has been damaged by shellfire

The first time we were in the trenches the Germans were only 60, or 70 yds away but we only had 2 casualties against about a dozen last time.

Lt A.J. Fraser, 3 January 1915

The trenches at night were a hive of activity, and sentries had to maintain a high level of alertness, even though their lack of sleep during the day would tempt them to nap – a military crime of a most serious nature. The cloying darkness seemed to magnify the noises that emanated from no man's land. As such, no man's land was regularly lit up brilliantly by flares, star shells fired by artillery, coloured warning rockets launched from the frontline, and smaller 'Very (or Verey) lights', the term originating from their American inventor, Edward W. Very. These flares were usually fired by officers from hand-held pistols, which threw up 'light balls' into the dark night sky.

From all sides darted flashes of brilliant fire, a perfect aurora of flame, silhouetting squat bushes, shattered tree trunks and pock-marked fields gleaming with water. In the sky gleamed dozens of brilliant blue lights, varied by showers of lovely golden balls.

Pte Arthur E. Lambert, 2nd Battalion,
Honourable Artillery Company

Opposite: Star shells and Very lights illuminate no man's land

Right: Firing a Very pistol at night

Working parties were also to move forward into the contested zone at night, to make repairs, carry out patrols and investigate suspicious objects. They had to be ever vigilant: star shells and Very lights would cause working parties to be starkly silhouetted against the skyline; warning rockets were fired to alert the artillery in case of attack. Opportunistic bursts of fixed machine guns were a threat – as were nervous sentries on one's own side.

Forward extensions of the trench systems were also created: saps dug out a short way into no man's land in order to give advance warning of impending attack. The forward trenches were protected by belts of barbed wire, an American invention that had seen some limited use in earlier wars, but which was to see its apogee in the Great War. Barbed wire was to form a significant component of the field defences and so it needed constant attention. Wiring parties on both

Barbed wire entanglements using silent screw pickets

sides entered no man's land under the cover of darkness: in patrols of two to three men to inspect the integrity of the defences or cut paths through their own wire in preparation for a raid; or, in larger fatigue parties (gangs of anywhere between twelve to eighty men), to repair and improve the frontline wire.

When you are out wiring you forget all about being in no man's land, unless the Germans are sniping across. The work is one that absorbs all your interest, and your one concern is to get the job done quickly and well.

Lt B. Adams, Royal Welsh Fusiliers, 1915

Wire was brought up the lines by fatigue parties who, usually under the instruction of a sapper officer or NCO, would carry out the work in darkness. Such parties would be in a constant state of readiness; any noise would trigger off a flurry of star shells and Very lights intended to illuminate the interlopers, picking them out in stark silhouette against the night sky, an easy target for a sweeping machine-gun fire or targeted artillery barrage. Private Groom of the London Rifle Brigade recalled the activity: 'the fear of noise, the desperate whisperings when the wire wouldn't roll, the ping of the wirecutter, the tin kicked in the dark.'

'Tap–tap–tap.' 'There's a wiring party out, sir. I've heard 'em these last five minutes.' Undoubtedly there are a few men out in no man's land, repairing the wire. I tell the sentries near to look out be ready to fire, and then I send off a 'Very' flare, fired by thick cartridge from a thick-barrelled brass pistol. It makes a good row, and has a fair kick, so it is best to rest the butt on the parapet and hold it at arm's length. Even so it leaves your ears singing for

hours. The first shot was a failure – only a miserable rocket tail which failed to burst. The second was a magnificent shot, it burst beautifully, and fell right behind the party, two Germans, and silhouetted them, falling and burning still incandescent on the ground behind.

Lt B. Adams, Royal Welsh Fusiliers, 1915

Wire picket

The more complex wire constructions involved the hammering in of wooden or angle-iron stakes by a maul; it was not surprising that soldiers feared the attention of the other side. The invention of the screw picket – which then spread like wildfire on both sides of no man's land – meant that complex wire barriers could be constructed relatively noiselessly, soldiers using their entrenching tool helves or other suitable post to wind them into the ground. The wire used by the British and German armies differed to a great extent: British wire was double strand with modest barbs; German wire, tough to work with, was single-strand, 2.5mm/sq. section wire with murderous barbs.

With the increased complexity of barbed wire came the increased necessity to cut it, if you weren't going to be left 'hanging on the old barbed wire' as one particularly fatalistic soldiers' song put it.

If you want to find the old battalion,
I know where they are, I know where they are,
I know where they are,
If you want to find the old battalion, I know
where they are,
They're hanging on the old barbed wire,
I've seen 'em, I've seen 'em, hanging on the old
barbed wire.
I've seen 'em, I've seen 'em, hanging on the old
barbed wire.

Soldiers' song, 1916

One's own wire was almost as hazardous as that of the enemy, and special paths had to be cut through the tangled maze of wires; lanes that could be targeted by enterprising machine gunners and snipers. To cut the enemy's wire was a hazardous job; wire

Opposite: Wiring parties had to await the cover of darkness to put in new pickets and repair the wire

Left: With barbed wire came the need to have wire cutters; those with long handles were the most effective

Below: Barbed wire cutter attachment for the SMLE rifle

would be attached to such warning signals as empty tin cans that would clatter alarmingly if the wire was touched. Early cutters were largely inadequate: Captain Siegfried Sassoon of the Royal Welsh Fusiliers would famously go in search of a decent pair from the Army and Navy Stores in London; 2nd Lieutenant Bruce Bairnsfather had to resort to French ironmongers with the same aim in mind. A great variety were tried and patented, and many tested in the Royal Engineers' experimental trench workshops. Makers Chatter Lea designed a variety of long-handled versions from 1917 that were more satisfactory, but still fraught with difficulties when it came to actually using the things.

Wire cutter attachments were made that were designed to be fixed to the muzzle of an infantryman's SMLE. These attachments were ungainly, designed to feed the wire onto jaws, which then pivoted when withdrawn to provide a cut. Given the great tangles encountered by the infantryman in action, these cutters were never really a practical proposition in the field. In most cases, cutting the wire was left to the artillery: a skilled business, it required shrapnel to burst at the correct height to obtain the right effect. History shows that this was not always achieved.

TRENCH LIFE

From the advent of trench warfare in late 1914, there emerged a routine that would come to encompass the world of the average soldier, a routine that would provide some order to an otherwise bizarre experience of living in a ditch, during which time the normal civilised code of activity during the day and rest during the night would become reversed. By day, soldiers would try to snatch some sleep while sentries were posted at box periscopes or their simple mirror equivalents, one per platoon, looking out for *Minenwerfer* (trench mortars), gas and unusual activity. By night, sentries would stand nervously on the fire-step, nervous in case of the casual and random play of a machine gun across no man's land. Between times, there would be inspections, trench repair and the issue of rations – brought up by rations carriers from the rear areas.

For both sides, trench routine usually commenced with 'stand-to' (from stand to arms) at one hour before dawn, when all troops in the frontline would stand upon the fire-step armed and ready to confront an attacker – the theory being that most attacks would take place at dawn. Stand-to would last at least an hour and a half, but would finish when the enemy parapet could be seen through the periscopes set up along the line of the trenches.

Stand-to was invariably accompanied by a fusillade of bullets fired off into the unknown space of no man's land. In what was often called the 'mad minute' or 'wind up', men would blast away to make their enemies aware of their existence.

Everyone stands to the parapet, and away to the left a tornado of crackling sound can be heard, getting louder and louder. In a few seconds it has swept down the line, and now a deafening rattle of rifle fire is going on immediately in front. Bullets are flicking the tops of the sandbags on the parapet in hundreds.

Capt. Bruce Bairnsfather, Royal Warwickshire Regiment

In some cases, artillery or *Minenwerfer* bombardments would accompany the small arms fire.

Visé Paris 763

Sketches of Tommy's life
Up the line — N° 5

The main duties in the Front Line in the daytime are watching the periscope, and looking up in the air for « trench mortars », with a whistle ready to blow for a warning.

F. Mackain

Watching for Minenwerfer was a constant part of trench life

I write you a few lines to say I'm still alive and well, although we are having it very stiff for fritzi straffs us every morning for we are in a very dangerous place.

Pte C.L. London, London Regiment, April 1917

This activity would soon die away, duty done, and peace would be resumed on both sides. Following stand-to, most men were stood down, leaving sentries on duty to man the fixed box periscopes. With stand-down and stand-to, a tot of rum would be issued to each man, a welcome respite from the often-freezing conditions at dawn and dusk. Its fiery warmth was intended to dispel some of the ague brought on by the cold, wet and miserable trench conditions. The issue of a rum ration in the armed forces was a British institution.

Service rum was thick and robust; its positive effects after a night on the fire-step are remembered in most soldiers' memoirs. Rum was issued from ceramic jugs labelled SRD. These initials spawned a host of jokey explanations, from 'Soon Runs Dry' to 'Seldom Reaches Destination'. An enduring mythology, the initials nevertheless stand for something rather more prosaic: 'Supply Reserve Depot', a large establishment based in Deptford, repository of many such stores. Famously, it was also issued to those men about to

Clockwise from right: Box periscopes were often fixed into position and used by sentries; sacking or another means of disguising the box periscope was important if the mirrors were not going to receive the attention of snipers; the No. 9 box periscope, which was capable of being folded

THE OUTPOST

A British "Tommy" watching the enemy through his periscope

go 'over the bags', either at dawn with a large-scale attack, or at night prior to a raid. The rum ration was issued by a senior NCO, under close inspection of an officer, the fiery effect of this viscous liquid being a boon in the cold, damp conditions of the trench.

Given that drunkenness was a serious offence, the ration could not be accumulated and saved for later; poured into mug or mess tin top, it was to be drunk in the presence of the officer. It was a long-held belief that, like the issue of strawberry jam, any rum residue left in a jug was taken by the sergeant as a perk of his position. Soldiers were otherwise not entitled to alcohol in the trenches, although officers' messes were to receive such precious liquids from home.

Breakfast followed stand-to, with the meal comprising rations that had been brought up at night, which were meant to last a forty-eight-hour period.

No matter how violent, sulphurous, or bloody the night, no matter how tense the grim ceremonial of 'stand to' which ushered in the day, the command 'stand down' was almost invariably followed by a lull along the line. Hostilities were temporarily suspended by mutual, if mute, consent … For anything from an hour to two hours the most vicious noise to be heard in the trench was the sizzling of frying bacon. Then, some machine gunner, cheerful from his meal, would break the spell with the

Sketches
of Tommy's life
Up the line — N° 7

One of the bright spots in our life.

Visé Paris 763

Issuing the rum ration

Your health !

We had our tea out in the garden to day,
as we used to do at home.

'pop-pop-pop-pop-pop!' call on his Vickers, which never failed to evoke the slower 'pop-pop' from some heavy machine-gun in the German lines.

Lt Sydney Rogerson, West Yorkshire Regiment, 1916

Tea, bacon, bread – these were the staples of trench food, but often it could be simply bully beef and biscuits. Food was a difficult issue for High Command: tinned food was relatively plentiful, but 'bully beef' – ration corned beef imported from South America – was hardly warming in the cold of Flanders and was not well received by the soldiers themselves.

I shall be glad when its over, have bully & biscuits, jam, tea, potatoes & seldom butter nothing else for the last month getting tired of this menu.

Pte Ted Carter, London Regiment, 47th Division, 23 May 1916

To relieve the monotony, and give sustenance to the men in the frontline, ration parties would bring up rations at night – usually men 'out at rest' detailed for work up the line who returned to their rest camps at night. With increasing sophistication of the military machine, hot rations in specially designed ration carriers were brought up the line; negotiating long communication trenches in the dark meant that this was often an arduous duty, but one much appreciated by the frontline troops all the same.

The rations' carriers was a most unenviable task, as thankless as it was dangerous. Rarely in those days did they complete their double journey without casualties. Occasionally the whole party was wiped out while the company waited, parched and famished, for the water and food scattered about the mud and shell-holes. Water was more precious even than victuals. It was everywhere 'but not a drop to drink,' while the full petrol tins were cruel burdens to shoulder over a mile or so of battle-field.

Lt Sidney Rogerson, West Yorkshire Regiment, 1916

All other rations would be brought up in sandbags, often in a hopeless jumble of loose tea, sugar, bread, bacon and tinned rations, intended for a forty-eight-hour period. Besides bully beef, other tinned food staples included 'pork and beans' (beans with a small cube of pork fat at the bottom of the tin) and the universal Maconochie ration (a vegetable and meat concoction that at least served to break the monotony

Opposite: Biscuits and jam

Left: Rations more often than not involved Fray Bentos bully beef, issue biscuits and plum & apple jam

of bully beef). Jam – 'pozzy' in soldier's slang – was another welcome ration; but the frequency of Tickler's Plum & Apple variety raised the eternal question: 'When the 'ell is it going to be Strawberry?' Fresh rations – meat, bacon, vegetables – would also be supplied, brought to the front in the ubiquitous sandbag.

Braziers – buckets with holes punched in them – were a means of keeping warm, as well as cooking, but their glow could be seen for some distance. Cooking in the trenches required some nerve. Too much smoke and the enemy guns could rain down a fusillade of 'whizz-bangs' – high-velocity shells – or send over 'minnies', the much-feared *Minenwerfer* trench mortars, capable of destroying sections of trenches and their occupants. Small fires were used for frying

bacon, heating Maconochie rations or brewing tea; braver souls in quieter sectors used braziers fuelled with issues of coke or, more often, pieces of broken trench boards. Private Groom of the London Rifle Brigade was impressed by an 'old sweat's' approach: using a candle stub, cigarette tin and 'four be' two' flannel, water could be boiled, slowly, enough for a mug of hot 'char'. Most coveted was the paraffin-fuelled Primus pressure stove, a sophisticated and efficient piece of engineering invented in the late nineteenth century – a rare luxury in the trenches.

For the soldier in the frontline, water was supplied in petrol tins, carried to the front by ration parties. As Shell Oil was the main supplier of fuel to the British Army, Shell petrol tins were undoubtedly seen in the frontline as water carriers. Unfortunately, the water would never quite lose its petrol taste – something even the strongest tea could not defeat. As recalled by Harry Patch, the last surviving veteran of the trenches, it was a standing joke that frontline soldiers could distinguish water from Shell or BP tins. Rum jars were also used for water when empty – it is presumed with a more palatable undertaste. Mineral waters and sodas sent from home – Schweppes bottles were common in the trenches – also provided some respite from the usual petrol-tainted water.

After breakfast, it was time for platoon commanders to make their inspection of rifles.

Pork and beans – a ration comprising beans with pork fat

At 5.30 'Stand down and clean rifles' is the order given, and the cleaning commences – a process as oft-repeated as 'washing up' in civilised lands, and as monotonous and unsatisfactory, for a few hours later the rifles are a bit rusty and muddy again, and need another inspection.

Lt B. Adams, Royal Welsh Fusiliers, 1915

*Clockwise from left:
Cooking in the trenches:
a brazier; heating
Maconochie rations in a
Dixie lid; dishing out the
rations into a mess tin*

Right: Mess tin lids and re-used rum jars, in this case containing fresh water rations

Below: Bread and issue spoons

Cleaning rifles in the muddy conditions during the winter months – or even when the mud had dried to dust in the summer months – was a major challenge for all men in the trenches. Officers' attentions were focused on breech and chamber, parts of the gun liable to fouling from mud and dirt, a significant issue in the muddy trenches of the Ypres Salient.

Some men were stuck in mud up to their chests all night. Where we were it varied from ankle to waist deep. It is difficult keeping rifles clean enough to use in such mud.

Lt A.J. Fraser, 3 January 1915

Such fouling would put paid to the delicate mechanism of the Canadian Ross Rifle, replaced from 1916 by the Lee–Enfield in Canadian service.

With rifles cleaned and inspected, and the men fed, those not on 'sentry-go' were detailed for fatigues to repair trenches and engage in similar activities. These activities would go on throughout the day, only broken for lunch at midday – drawing upon the rations brought up to the frontline – and an evening meal at around 6 p.m. No soldiers in their right minds would place themselves at risk by moving around the frontline in daytime, and reminders (in the form of trench signs) of trenches requiring repair and dangerous corners were strategically

Sketches
of Tommy's life
Up the line — N° 4

The only time I ever saw a man cry was when one of our chaps dropped his rifle in the mud after spending exactly two hours cleaning it.

Visé Paris 763

Cleaning rifles in the muddy conditions was challenging

Soldiers cleaned themselves up in the frontline when they had a chance after stand-down. Shaving was often done in the dregs of tea

placed in order to save soldiers' lives from snipers, and from those taking random pot shots. Soldiers had to be vigilant at all times.

Looking over the parapet in daylight was most unwise: snipers would have weapons fixed in position, targeted at dips in the parapet, at latrines and crossing points, and at loophole plates.

There was a tingle in the air; everything was as still as death; the sun was shining from a very blue sky, and throwing longer and longer shadows in the snow as the afternoon wore on. It was a valuable afternoon, the enemy's wire showing up clearly against the white ground, and I was showing the new snipers how to search the trench systematically from left to right, noting the exact position of anything that looked like a loop-hole, or steel-plate, and especially the thickness of the wire, what kind, and whether it was great and new, or rusty-red and old; whether there were any gaps in it, and where.

Lt B. Adams, Royal Welsh Fusiliers, 1915

There was continual loss of life on the Western Front through the actions of snipers in this way, combined with the altogether random attentions of the artillery shell.

From early on, the need to be able to look over the parapet to observe activity in no man's land led to the production of specially designed 'trench periscopes'. In an issue of the *Transactions of the Optical Society* for 1915, the basic parameters were laid down for trench periscopes, the object of which, it was stated, was 'to give the soldier a view of his front whilst his head and person are sheltered'.

Many patent versions were produced to try to achieve these aims: several of them were adopted officially; others were available for private purchase. For portability, a simple mirror attached to a stick or bayonet was the most effective. For 2nd Lieutenant Bernard Martin, such contrivances were more effective than larger box periscopes, which were much more susceptible to damage from shellfire, and its simple cover sufficient to keep off the rain. More commonly, day sentries would be at station next to a No. 9 box periscope, which was in the form of a collapsible and reasonably portable simple wooden box over 25in long (to provide the shelter required), and with a clear field of view sufficient for most trench duties. As the top mirror was susceptible to sniping, care was taken to protect the observer from glass splinters. Although portable, such periscopes were fixed at sentry posts throughout frontline trenches, effectively disguised from sniping by the use of sandbags and sacking.

Officers were drawn to more portable periscopes and, early on in the war, the 'Lifeguard' trench periscope, manufactured and patented by the Manchester firm of F. Duerrs, was widely advertised in the press. This periscope was constructed on the expanding 'lazy tong' principle, which when extended provided the required two opposed mirrors separated by 2ft; when collapsed the device was only 2in deep. The commonest periscope used by officers was the Beck's No. 25, issued from 1917, which comprised a simple small-diameter brass tube, with detachable handle and a focusing eyepiece. This effective piece of equipment was not only light, durable and difficult to spot at a distance, and long enough to provide the observer with sufficient protection, it was also a magnifying periscope.

Right: Sniping required attention to detail; snipers at loophole plates had to be careful that light did not show through the loophole, and used blankets or other covers to disguise them

Below: The simplest periscopes were mirrors attached to bayonets, or to twigs on the parapet

With sniping a constant menace, steel helmets were an innovation intended to combat its effects. In 1914, all armies were equipped with some form of uniform cap or ceremonial helmet, the German *Pickelhaube* being an example of this type – gaudy, impractical and affording little protection from either the elements or bullets. Up until 1915, Tommy was to wear the Service Dress cap in all its forms in the frontline. In action, this meant that head wounds were common, especially in its static phases when the attention of snipers was concentrated on the movement of soldiers past loopholes and dips in the trench sides. Soldiers were vulnerable to snipers, but they were also subject to the random tragedies of spent bullets, and from air-burst shrapnel and shell fragments. Clearly there was a need for increased head protection, and this was to be introduced in late 1915, with innovation by the French, Germans and British producing markedly different steel helmets.

The British helmet was invented by John Brodie and was pressed from non-magnetic steel, its dish-like form and wide brim intended to supply protection from above – hence the widespread use of the term 'shrapnel helmet'. The real innovation, it was claimed, was the liner, which provided space between the head and the helmet, allowing for dents and dings without impacting with the cranium. The helmet had two prototype designs, varying in the depth of its bowl and the width of its rim; the first official helmet, the War Office Pattern, was introduced in 1915 and possessed a sharp, unprotected rim. Problems with the sharpness of its rim, and the smooth reflective surface of the helmet (and complaints to that effect from General Plumer), led to the introduction of an improved helmet, known as the Mark I, which had a steel protective rim added, and a non-reflective sand finish. In most cases, the distinctive silhouette of the 'tin hat' was disguised by sacking or sandbags in close-fitting covers, while some battalions painted divisional signs or attached regimental badges to their helmets or covers.

Officers frequently used their own privately purchased helmets, with expensive liners fitted in fashionable outfitters. Prior to the widespread introduction of the Brodie helmet, officers purchased other patterns of helmet, such as the single-piece, hardened-steel *Acier Tempe* helmet, which resembled the stylish but complex Adrian helmet issued to French troops in 1915. Other, fluted helmets were also in relatively wide circulation, sometimes with a rakish leather band around the base.

Back in the trenches, the night routine would commence with another 'stand-to' before dusk, and another officers' inspection. The trenches then came alive to a routine of repair, supply and patrol; with men engaged on endless trench improvement, and with patrols and wiring parties out in no man's land, keeping an eye out for star shells that could catch them starkly silhouetted against the sky, targets for watchful sentries and searching machine guns.

The three subalterns in A Company took turns at duty in the trenches, four hours on and eight hours off, night and day. The duty consisted chiefly of visiting the sentries every hour, and keeping a general look-out, and seeing that the trench rules were obeyed. A good deal of rifle fire went on at night. Sentries on either side would exchange shots, and an occasional machine-gun would open out. At close range the bullets make a curious crack as they pass overhead. Being tall and having been warned of the efficiency of the German sniper, I had to walk in most of the trenches with a bend in the back, which soon became tiring.

Capt. Francis Buckley, 7th Battalion, Northumberland Fusiliers

Night sentries, with a round in the chamber ready for an alert, were detailed to look over the parapet – a dangerous act when the enemy had his guns trained at head height for the same reason.

The last twenty-four hours have really been a blank – the usual rounds at night, visiting sentries, the usual slipping and stumbling over abandoned trenches and mud-holes in the dark, the usual stand to arms at daybreak, and then sleep.

Lt A.D. Gillespie, Argyll and Sutherland Highlanders, April 1915

An officer's periscope, the 'Lifeguard', and the Becks tubular periscope

Sleeping on sentry duty was a capital offence; experienced NCOs made it their business to visit their charges every fifteen minutes, and officers would also be vigilant in their duties. Other men not on duty would be allowed to sleep, if they were lucky, or be ordered to go on endless carrying details, bringing up supplies from the rear along communication trenches. Supplying the trenches was a truly prodigious effort in the often-congested areas.

With trenches under continuous, random bombardment, trench boards, duckboards and revetments needed continuous upkeep. With men 'out on rest' bringing supplies to the reserve trenches, more often than not it would be the frontline troops who would have to ensure they were delivered to their destinations, and who would have to work to improve the lot of the trenches, or to go out under the cover of darkness to repair the wire.

A 'working party' usually consists of seventy to a hundred men from a company, with either one or two officers. The Brigadier going round the trenches finds a communication trench falling in, and about a foot of mud at the bottom. 'Get a working-party on this at once,' he says to his Staff Captain. The Staff Captain consults one of his R.E. officers, and a note is sent to the Adjutant of one of the two battalions in billets: 'Your battalion will provide a working party of ... officers ... full ranks (sergeants and corporals) and ... other ranks tomorrow. Report to Lt. ... R.E., at ... 5.00 pm tomorrow for work on ... trench. Tools will be provided.

Lt B. Adams, Royal Welsh Fusiliers, 1915

If the day-to-day life of the trenches was costly in materiel, then preparations for an attack saw supply issues on a huge scale – especially in the period before the British offensive on the Somme in July 1916. In just one small sector of the Somme battlefront, that of the 9th Brigade (3rd Division) at Carnoy, some 5,000 grenades, 1,600 trench mortar rounds, 1,400 ration boxes, 368 boxes of SAA ammunition (for rifles and machine guns) and 330 tins of water had to be carried up the line from the supply dump to be in place two days before the battle.

Mark I steel helmets with Machine Gun Corps insignia; such insignia were sometimes attached to the helmet shell or cloth cover

'War Office Pattern' steel helmet belonging to Lieutenant Terence Honychurch. Commissioned from the ranks in October 1915, Lieutenant Honychurch died on 22 September 1916 while serving with the Middlesex Regiment (57th Foot). This helmet has an officer's private purchase line, to improve fit

of light and, for the most part, this was obtained through the use of the humble candle. For the average soldier, possession of candle stubs provided both light and a rudimentary means of cooking or, at very least, in the hands of an experienced soldier, the boiling of the water for tea. Light was also a comfort, particularly in the underground world of the dugouts, and candles would be requested in parcels sent from home.

Bankier is a sort of Wm. Whiteley, whose parcels contain everything from cigars to carriage candles. Please don't think this is a hint that I want either, for I will let you know when my supply of Sunderland candles begins to run short.

Lt A.D. Gillespie, Argyll and Sutherland Highlanders, March 1915

Carrying such materiel, even in the best of conditions, was back-breaking work; even more so if the landscape was churned up by war.

Fifty yards on a good road is quite far enough for a box of 'ammo'. That distance on a week-old battlefield is like ten miles. Men slid all over the place. First one foot went down, then the other. Frequent falls were complete and man and box came down with a crash.

Pte Arthur E. Lambert, 2nd Battalion, Honourable Artillery Company

As the trenches came alive at night, with a host of activity from trench repairs to sorties out into no man's land, it was necessary to provide some form

Candles could also be obtained from the Expeditionary Force Canteen, the YMCA and other charitable organisations set up to administer to the needs of the troops, and were often exchanged between soldiers coming in and out of the line. Birmingham manufacturers the Albion Lamp Co. created a series of mild steel cases for candles, as well as folding candle lanterns that fitted into a steel carry case. Care had to be taken to ensure that such lights did not bring down a hail of artillery, a *Minenwerfer* attack, or the sweep of a machine gun.

It was mandatory that web equipment be worn in the trenches; it could only be removed, temporarily, when visiting the latrine. Despite this, it was rare indeed that the full equipment set would be worn; instead, the large pack (containing greatcoat and a range of other items) would be sent back with the battalion transport. The full equipment set was known as 'marching order'; when in the frontline, the

*Sentry duty: SMLE with
bayonet fixed and Webley
Mark VI in a trench*

At a bombing post: open grenade box and SMLE. The soldier's respirator is nearby, in its satchel

small pack would be transferred to the back, redistributing the weight of the set, in what became known as 'battle order'. Officers too would be encumbered with a variety of kit in the frontline.

Still half asleep, I struggled into the clothes I was to wear for three days. I put on trench boots, donned a heavy cardigan, decorated with woolly mascots, under my khaki jacket, and a leather jerkin above it. Over all I buckled on the various items of my 'Christmas tree' – gas respirator, water bottle, revolver and haversack – took a rolled-up ground-sheet instead of an overcoat, wound a knitted scarf round my neck and exchanged my cap for a 'battle bowler'.

Lt S. Rogerson, West Yorkshire Regiment, 1916

As such, trenches were modified so that men could reach their equipment more efficiently – and particularly to access ammunition. In the frontline, soldiers had to carry 150 rounds of small arms ammunition (SAA) in their pouches, forming their reserve and their primary source of ammunition when in action. The standard bullet was the .303in-calibre Mark VII infantry bullet (pointed and thus distinguished from the older Mark VI, which was used by the navy and Territorial battalions still employing the 'long' Lee–Enfield pattern rifle). Bullets were issued in cotton bandoliers holding five chargers of five rounds each, and these bandoliers were packed in ammunition boxes – an open box of which was kept in each fire-bay (although the authorities frowned upon the draping of bandoliers from appropriate points in the trenches as being untidy).

The primary purpose of trenches was to provide cover and concealment for the men who occupied them. Living in open ditches in all weathers was trying, especially as artillery fire was concentrated upon opposing trenches in order to destroy them and their occupants. With most men killed or wounded by artillery fire, the only sure protection was to take men out of the line and into underground shelters, or dugouts. Building dugouts presented the opportunity to exploit the many feet of soil or rock that nature had provided as a means of protection against the searching activities of shellfire, and provided a respite for men in the frontline attempting to gain some rest, as well as a means of escaping the worst of the weather conditions.

My dearest John,

Thank you so much for your beautifully written letter, which came to me here in the trenches. I am living in a little cave just behind the trenches. They call it a dug-out, and it is very like a rabbit's burrow. Every now and then I go through a little passage into the trench to have a look through a spy-hole at mister German, but he is very careful and does not show himself much, as he is frightened Daddy might shoot him.

Col Ruddles-Brise, Essex Regiment, writing to his son, 11 February 1915

Sketches
of Tommy's life
Up the line — N° 6

On Sentry Go at Night.

F. Mackain

Sentry duty at night, peering out into no man's land

Candles were an important commodity in the trenches. Commercial manufacturers supplied a need, such as this Khaki Kombination Kandlebox, which contained a candle and holder, the box shielding the light when opened

Early war, dugouts were little more than scrapes in the trench walls; known universally as 'funk-holes', they actually provided little opportunity for protection, and little chance of rest. Deeper dugouts were initially frowned upon by the British, who felt that soldiers might become reliant upon them and might not wish to leave them. Common sense prevailed, fortunately, and deeper dugouts started appearing in the British lines from the end of 1915, for accommodation, headquarters space, and regimental aid posts. The German lines, organised for defence and destined to be there for some time, had always had such protection – particularly in the drier chalk ground of Artois and Picardy.

It was the first deep dugout I had entered, and of course it was the work of the Germans. There were about twenty steps down at either end, the wooden sides of the stairway scarred with bullet holes and splinters. Inside there were just two narrow apartments, one for our bedroom and the other for meals. Though rather draughty it was comfortable enough and practically shell-proof.

Capt. Francis Buckley, 7th Battalion, Northumberland Fusiliers

Dugouts quickly became cluttered with officers' possessions – maps, weapons, trench orders, communication equipment and a plethora of other materiel – while at the surface the individual soldier's ingenuity was hastily turned to new ways of making their lot easier in the frontline.

I noticed as I passed along that the trenches were not only beginning to look more efficient as defences, but more lived in, more 'homely'. German bayonets stuck in the walls served as pegs for bandoliers of cartridges, water bottles, and other parts of his complex harness which Mr Atkins was accustomed to take off in the trenches. Here and there hung a gas-gong in the shape of a brass shell-case.

Lt S. Rogerson, West Yorkshire Regiment, 1916

Increasingly, the military mind was turned to improving the efficiency of day-to-day trench warfare, its protocols and structures. Committees were established to examine the efficiency of the trench system of working and, locally, officers set about improving their lot and creating order from chaos. The man in the trenches also sought ways of developing his own comfort zone: on the lookout for incoming trench mortars and gas shells (which made a peculiar 'plopping' sound) in his patch of sky; making the best of a bad job. Commercial manufacturers also very quickly cottoned on to the opportunity to market products aimed at the men in the frontline, selling goods that were fit 'for the trenches', whatever they may have been. Some of these made their way into parcels sent from home: rudimentary cooking devices such as 'Tommy cookers' (using solid fuel), candle boxes or 'trench' writing sets.

In fact, the prefix 'trench' was added to everything: trench stores, trench boots, trench cap, trench foot, trench fever, trench boards, and so on. Of these, trench foot and trench fever were ailments peculiar to those living in damp ditches in close association with hundreds of other unwashed bodies, day after day.

Opposite: German shoulder straps were often captured during
trench raids; these were important for identifying the enemy
occupying the opposing trenches

Below: Peering into an officer's dugout, c.1916

Shortly before Xmas we were in the trenches again … One man in my squadron was killed & 5 others wounded while a good many including myself got our feet more or less frostbitten, having been so much under water in this weather.

Lt A.J. Fraser, 3 January 1915

Trench foot was a condition caused by prolonged immersion of the feet in water or liquid mud. A significant commitment to its prevention was required if men were not to be eventually hospitalised. In the absence of trench waders or other forms of rubber boots, constant care of the feet, including inspections, manipulation with whale oil and frequent changes of socks, was necessary – and was constantly advertised to the rank and file by the staff.

Trench feet, one lecture always began, 'is that state produced by excessive cold or long standing in water or liquid mud.' We soon got to know too much, we felt, about the use of whale-oil and anti-frostbite grease, the changing of socks and the rubbing and stamping of feet.

Lt B. Adams, Royal Welsh Fusiliers, 1915

Trench fever was a viral disease usually classified at the time as 'pyrexia of unknown origin'. Suffering extreme fevers, with high temperatures and all that goes with such symptoms, men with trench fever were often hospitalised. Unidentified at the time, a link was made post-war with the bites of body lice – the inevitable consequence of confining so many men in difficult conditions. The adult body louse (*Pediculus vestimenti* in Latin) has a lifespan of around four weeks, and lives clinging to the undergarments, close enough to the skin in order to feed while still attached to the cloth, its frequent feeding causing great discomfort, sores and, eventually, infections. Gathered in the warmth of the seams of the woollen uniforms, and clustered in the intimate parts of the soldiers' bodies, lice multiplied rapidly and spread from man to man.

Tommy would resort to removal of the 'chats' by hand, running the fingernail through seams or playing a candle flame along them, and hearing the insects 'pop' (but thereby weakening uniforms). Commercial powders – such as Keatings – were considered to be practically useless by soldiers, who soundly believed it to encourage the vermin to multiply. Nonetheless, such treatments were sent regularly from home.

On average, men spent a period of four to eight days in the frontline, but this depended very much on circumstance, with some battalions spending longer in hard-pressed areas. Private Herbert Mason of the 6th Battalion, Oxfordshire and Buckinghamshire Light Infantry clandestinely recorded his trench duties while serving in the 20th (Light) Division at Ypres. In 1915–16, his tours of the trenches lasted between four and eleven days in the Salient, and this was typical of many. While some men were in the front fire trenches, others would occupy the support lines behind, ready to provide reinforcement when hard pressed in an attack or raid.

There was to be a rhythm to trench warfare, with typically five days in the frontline, five in reserve, five at the front again and, finally, five days in reserve. Relief, when it came, saw the battalion removed from the frontline trenches and taken to the rear areas, where they would be billeted in farm buildings, and where they could receive pay and were able to buy such comforts as *oeuf-frites*, *café-au-lait* and beer. During this period, reinforcements and replacements for losses sustained would arrive; men would be trained in the use of new weapons, gas procedures and other aspects of the evolving war.

Dear Kitty.
I have been up the line and have come down to base for rest. I received your letter the day I went up the line. I have had no time to write to before because we have been after old Fritz as been retreating ever since we went into the line. We followed him up for about six mile and he kept *running away all the time he caught a few of our chaps with is Artillery and our artillery knocked many of his out well.*

Pte Percy Edwards, 17 Battalion, Royal Welsh Fusiliers, September 1918

Maps, compasses, messages

SIX "KAMPITE" Trench Fuel Blocks
PATENT
COMPLETE WITH STAND
EACH BLOCK WILL BURN
CAN BE USED IN DUG-OUTS, TENTS, AND TRENCHES.
9D
FOR FIFTEEN MINUTES
NON-EVAPORATING SAFE, CLEAN ECONOMICAL.

"KAMPITE" SAFETY TRENCH COOKER.
DIRECTIONS FOR USE.
PLACE A BLOCK ON THE GROUND, OR ON A PIECE OF METAL OR OTHER NON-FLAMMABLE MATERIAL.
OPEN STAND TO FORM A TRIANGLE. LIGHT THE WICK AT BOTH ENDS, AND PLACE PUT STAND IN POSITION.
KETTLE OR SAUCEPAN ON STAND.
A BLOCK BURNS FOR FIFTEEN MINUTES.
"KAMPITE" FUEL DOES NOT LIQUIFY OR EVAPORATE, AND CAN BE USED ALMOST ANYWHERE.
A SINGLE BLOCK CAN BE CARRIED IN THE POCKET WITH PERFECT SAFETY.

B FAA 261801

WEAPONS OF WAR

The Great War is closely connected with the development of weapons designed to inflict the maximum loss of life on the protagonists. Of these weapons, it is perhaps the machine guns that are most associated with the reign of death on the battlefield, and they were certainly effective in scything through the attacking formations – so much so that gallantry medals were often awarded for the capture or destruction of machine-gun posts. It is not surprising that the armies were at pains to disguise them.

Despite the power of the machine gun, however, it was probably artillery fire that was most feared, its devastating effects evident in the destruction of the landscape, and in the often random deaths caused by the explosion of shells of all calibres. Artillery fire became increasingly sophisticated as the war progressed; with timed barrages designed to 'lift', maintaining a rolling effect in front of an advance, or the isolation of raiding parties in box barrages, deterring the enemy from attacking by walls of shells. Trench maps and other innovations were a result of the need to accurately place shellfire, and a complex system of grid coordinates was evolved to achieve this. The gunners were constant companions in arms to the infantry, providing barrage fire at the opening of offensives, and being frequently called upon, through signal flares and fragile telephone lines, to deal with troublesome machine-gun nests, snipers and suspicious activity in no man's land.

The British Army went to war with the machine gun as a specialist weapon; two heavy Vickers machine guns being allocated to each infantry battalion. As no one had expected the war to be a static one – with an increased role for the machine gun in both defence (protecting a position) and attack (creating a barrage) – this was hardly surprising. Yet machine gunners were to become an elite arm. The power of the British Vickers Mark I machine gun and its German MG08 Maxim equivalent was truly frightening. Fired in short bursts of 200 rounds per minute (although they had a rate of fire of 450 rounds per minute), both guns had a maximum effective range of 2,000yds – accuracy and hit rate increasing as the range decreased. With deeper considerations of machine-gun tactics came the idea that the Vickers guns should be taken away from infantry battalions and given, in larger numbers, to the newly formed Machine Gun Corps (MGC). In this way, the role of MGC was guided by divisional commanders, in order that it might provide effective infantry support. In return for their loss, infantry battalions were issued with the lighter Lewis Gun, more suited to an infantry role.

The Lewis guns had only recently become company weapons, and were still somewhat of a novelty … Alan arrived, with one of the team carrying two spare drums of ammunition. We pointed out the spot, and he laid his gun on the parapet, with the butt against his shoulder and his finger on the trigger, and waited. 'Flash!' 'There he is, sir!' from the sentry. 'Drrrrrr-r-r-r:' purred the Lewis gun, then stopped. Then again, ending with another jerk. There was silence.

Lt B. Adams, Royal Welsh Fusiliers, 1915

Men deemed proficient in handling both Vickers and Lewis machine guns were awarded badges to be worn on the right lower sleeve: MG for machine

Opposite: 'Kampite', a commercially produced solid fuel cooker 'can be used in dug-outs, tents and trenches'

Service Dress insignia from the uniform of Lance Corporal John Carruthers, Border Regiment. Carruthers served with the 17th Division, was wounded twice, and was a qualified machine gunner in both Vickers (MG) and Lewis (LG). He survived the war

Opposite, top: the Vickers in position. Bottom: Covering a Vickers from the elements

gunner, LG for Lewis gunner. In some cases, unofficial or division-specific machine-gun flashes were also worn on the sleeve. The MGC itself was to wear a cap badge of crossed Vickers machine guns.

Trench mortarmen – TMs or 'toc emmas', in the phonetic alphabet of the day – were described as the 'suicide club'; a group of soldiers who were likely as not to be targeted for retaliatory action by their opposite numbers in the enemy trenches. For this reason, among many others, TMs were unpopular in the frontline. Trench mortars – simple trench-scale

artillery capable of firing high-trajectory shells or bombs – were to become increasingly sophisticated as the war proceeded, and were used as a means of destroying or reducing enemy trenches, for they were capable of killing large numbers of men in any trench. The German equivalent – the *Minenwerfer* – was especially feared.

The British experimented with a variety of contraptions – including catapults firing grenades – but the first effective mortars started to appear in 1915. These included the 'toffee apple', or 2in medium trench mortar, introduced in mid-1915. It comprised a 42lb spherical bomb containing the explosive charge (ammonal, identified by a pink band, or amatol, a green one) that was mounted on a long shaft. It was fired from a 2in-diameter tube, and was liable to destabilise in flight. A single round could destroy 6 sq./yds of barbed wire.

Perhaps more reliable was the Stokes mortar, a simple 3in drainpipe affair that was effectively the prototype for mortars in use in armies across the world today. Stokes bombs were dropped into the tube, a striker activating the charge and propelling the round up to 1,500yds. Stokes mortar bombs today litter the former battlefields in out-of-the-way places; unstable still, they remain volatile, a deadly echo of a past war. Stokes TM batteries, organised from 1915, were formed from infantrymen who wore blue flaming grenade sleeve insignia – distinguishing them from battalion bombers, who wore similar, red, grenades. Medium and heavy trench mortars were produced from 1916 to 1917, and were manned by artillerymen.

As the war progressed, it was the hand grenade – or bomb, as it was most commonly referred to – that was to largely replace the rifle as the primary offensive weapon of trench warfare. It required little training to use (although fatal accidents were common) and, placed correctly, grenades had a wide kill radius that was more efficient than the well-placed shot of even the most skilled marksman. As the conflict continued, so did bombing tactics: grenade assaults on frontline trenches were led by 'bayonet men' with the bombers and their grenade carriers following; behind them were 'sandbag men', whose role was to block off sections of trench won in the assault. In this way, frontline trenches were often shared by enemies, with only a bomb stop between them – a precarious state of affairs.

Despite this eventual sophistication, the British Army went to war with an extremely cumbersome grenade – the Mark I. The Mark I was a 16in stick grenade with a cast-iron explosive chamber and streamers to make it stable in flight. But the Mark I had a fatal flaw – it was detonated by a percussion striker, which meant that the bomber had to be extremely careful not to hit the side of the trench when preparing to throw it – a difficult proposition given the length of the handle. This, together with difficulties of supply, meant that by 1915 soldiers were making their own, ignited by a slow-burning fuse – usually at the rate of 1in of fuse per 1.25 seconds of delay.

Typical of these emergency bombs is the 'jam-tin' bomb – literally a tin filled with explosive gun cotton and shrapnel balls – that is particularly associated with the Gallipoli Campaign of 1915. Versions of the same grenade, attached to a wooden handle, are known to have been produced to improve the throwing distance; other types of 'hair brush' grenade carried blocks of explosive. Unwieldy, these were used ultimately for attacking dugouts. Another locally made grenade, the 'Battye bomb' – so named after its inventor, Major Basil Battye RE – was manufactured locally at Béthune, and consisted of a cast-iron cylinder containing 40g of explosive, sealed with a wooden stopper and ignited by a Nobel fuse – activated by a friction cap.

The Lewis light machine gun in position

The No. 15 was the first grenade to be mass-produced, again in 1915. Resembling a cricket ball, it could be thrown a reasonable distance, but with its simple cast-iron body and cord fuse it looked particularly archaic. Also ignited by friction, the No. 15 was badly affected by wet weather, the special friction brassards issued to bombers becoming useless – a factor that was to be a major problem in the Loos Campaign of September 1915. Although half a million grenades of this type were eventually produced, they were unreliable and were to decline in popularity with the introduction of the superior 'Mills bomb' from May 1915, named after its principle inventor William Mills.

Officially designated the No. 5 grenade, the secret of the Mills' success lay with its ignition system, which used a striker that was activated when a pin was removed and a lever released. The lever was then ejected and a four-second fuse activated, during which time the bomber had to throw the grenade. The body of the grenade was formed of cast iron, weighed 1¼lb, and its surface was divided into sections to promote fragmentation. Coloured bands indicated its fillings: pink for ammonal, green for amatol.

Hand grenades could only be thrown so far; rifle grenades, at first mistrusted by the War Office but accepted into service at the outbreak of war, could be propelled a greater distance, which was useful in positional warfare. Fired from a rifle loaded with a propellant cartridge (a normal .303 cartridge – minus the bullet – with 35 grains of cordite and a tuft of gun cotton), the No. 3 grenade (also known as the Hales, after its inventor) used a steel rod that was placed in the rifle barrel. A percussion grenade, it was filled with the explosive trotyl or, later, amatol or ammonal. An improved version, issued in 1916 (the No. 20 grenade), removed some of the complexities of the first pattern

Bomber and trench mortar qualification grenades, worn on the sleeve: red for bombers; blue for trench mortarmen

– such as a spring clip to grip the rifle muzzle, and a wind vane – but delivered a similar explosive punch.

The No. 23 grenade was a new pattern of Mills bomb, initially designed to be used as a rifle grenade, but later (with the Mark II) being used either as a hand-thrown bomb or, with the addition of a steel rod screwed into the base plug, a rifle grenade. A special cup was designed to keep the grenade in position for firing, and the bomb itself carried ammonal (marked with a pink band) or amatol (green band). A revised model, the No. 36, followed in 1917. The No. 36 was first filled with explosive and then dipped in shellac, a process that sealed the grenade and thus prevented rapid deterioration. Unlike its predecessor, the No. 36 was fired from a special 'cup discharger', and had a disc-like 'gas check' screwed into its base plate in order to ensure that all the propellant gases did their job.

'Toffee apple' mortars in position, waiting for fusing and firing

All Mills bombs were carried in boxes of twelve – the detonators were carried separately in a tin in the centre of the box, to avoid unnecessary accidents. Arming the grenade was a tricky business, and required the steady hand of a trained bomber. Battalion bombers were equipped with simple tools to enable them to remove the base plate and prime the grenade; hooks were also provided to bombing specialists to enable them to remove the pins quickly and efficiently, thereby increasing the rate of throw. It has been estimated that approximately 70 million Mills bombs were thrown by the Allies during the war, alongside at least 35 million other types, including many rifle grenades, a testimony to the importance of this weapon in trench warfare.

*The improvised
jam-tin bomb, filled
with explosive and
waste metal*

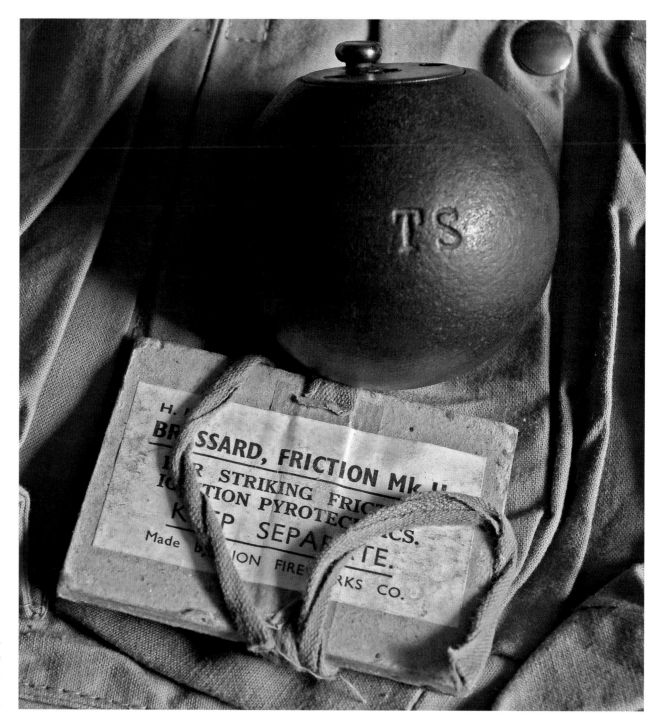

The No. 15 'cricket ball' grenade. This suffered from the elements, as it relied on the friction brassard to light its fuse

Beside me lay two bombers and a box of bombs: we were all peering out into a space that seemed enormous. Suddenly a German starlight rocketed up, and as it burst the great white bowl of the crater jumped into view. Then a few rifle shots sang across the gulf. There followed a deeper darkness than before.

Lt B. Adams, Royal Welsh Fusiliers, 1915

Gas warfare was to be deployed in an active sense in April 1915, when the Germans made the first practical use of cloud gas during the opening phases of the Second Battle of Ypres. Here, chlorine gas released from cylinders caused panic and fear among those who faced it, equipped only with wetted handkerchiefs. The French troops manning the frontline were overcome, with between 800 and 1,400 men killed, and a further 2,000–3,000 men injured. The line nevertheless held, and

the use of gas to achieve the much-anticipated 'breakthrough' was much diminished.

The British first used cloud gas to make good the deficiencies of the artillery preparations for the Battle of Loos, in September 1915. The chlorine gas – codenamed 'the accessory' for secrecy – that was to be used in the assault was to be the responsibility of the 'Special Companies' of the Royal Engineers, under the enthusiastic leadership of Major, later Lt-Colonel, C.H. Foulkes, RE. The original Special Companies were formed in Helfaut, south-east of St Omer, in July 1915, from men with specialist experience transferred from the infantry, and new companies were added right up to September that year. Those men with suitable experience – often chemistry graduates – were given the rank 'chemist corporal'. The Special Companies were distinguished by their multiple vertically striped pink, white and green armbands or brassards – indicating their authority to stay in the trenches during the assault.

Above, left to right: The No. 5 grenade, the Mills bomb; its pink band indicates filling with ammonal explosive; removing the pin meant that the spring-loaded striker lever had to be kept close to the bomb before throwing; after it was thrown, the lever flew off and the striker lit the fuse; the base plug had to be removed for priming the grenade

The No. 2 percussion grenade, a stick grenade with tonite explosive

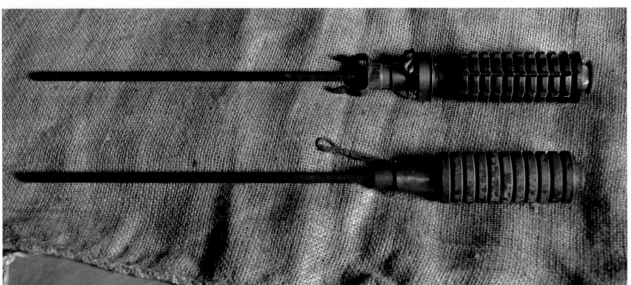

Rifle grenades: the No. 3 and its improved version, the No. 20

The gas was dispensed from cylinders fitted with flexible pipes that connected to the business end of the affair, a ½in-wide iron pipe that was up to 10ft long, and which was fitted with a jet at its end. The chlorine was released by the Special Company personnel upon receiving the order to proceed, through the simple act of turning on a stopcock. With the atmospheric conditions indifferent to an effective discharge, the gas did its work only in small parts of the line; elsewhere it had a negative effect on the British troops it was intended to support. Cloud gas release was initially a crude weapon, but by the end of the war gas warfare was more sophisticated, with many means of delivery in shells, mortars and grenades.

From late 1915, with the issue of effective respirators, gas was to become just another weapon to be endured by the man in the trenches. Primitive respirators were improvised in the early days, with General Headquarters of the British Expeditionary Force (BEF) issuing a directive that field dressings should be soaked in bicarbonate of soda, an alkaline, to combat the suspected chlorine – urine would also be called upon to do the same job. The 1st Canadian Division, on the right flank of the line, was attacked on 24 April 1915, but its protection was only to be wetted handkerchiefs and cotton bandoliers. Scientific advice mustered by the British was to devise a respirator around a pad of cotton waste soaked with sodium hyposulphite, sodium carbonate and glycerine, which was held in black mourning gauze, used to tie the mask to the face. The resulting War Office Black Veiling Respirator was to save many lives in May of 1915. It was still inadequate, however; under pressure of attack, the veiling could not be tied easily, and it only gave protection for a limited period.

A replacement was desperately needed. The first to arrive, in May 1915, was a flannel hood designed by Captain Cluny MacPherson of the Newfoundland Regiment. The hood covered the whole head, its tail being tucked into the tunic to provide a seal. A simple mica window was provided for vision. The 'Hypo Helmet' (officially, Smoke Helmet) was soaked in sodium hyposulphite, and protection given by the fact that the 'hypo' solution would counteract the gas drawn in through the material by the process of breathing.

Then about six o'clock the bombardment got louder, and our guns woke up like fun. 'Vee-bm … vee-bm' from our whizz-bangs going over, and then the machine-guns began on our left. Simultaneously, in came Richards (Dixon's servant) with an excited air. 'Gas,' he exclaimed. Instinctively I felt for my gas helmet.

Lt B. Adams, Royal Welsh Fusiliers, 1915

By the autumn of 1915, at the time of Loos, the Hypo Helmet had been replaced by a more sophisticated version, the 'Phenate (P) Helmet', which used the same basic gas hood design. This was developed in response to the proliferation of gas types, particularly phosgene, ten times more toxic than chlorine. This mask was soaked in sodium phenate, and was made from cotton flannelette (as wool flannel was rotted by the phenate), with two circular glass eyepieces, and a tube valve to expel carbon dioxide held in the teeth, with a rubber outlet. This nightmarish creation, also known as the tube helmet, would be famously recorded as the 'goggle-eyed bugger with the tit' by Captains Robert Graves and J.C. Dunn of the Royal Welsh Fusiliers. It would be used, rolled up in readiness on the head, with the Hypo Helmet

Clockwise from right: A bomber's post; priming No. 23 Mark II grenades; priming the No. 36 Mills grenade; Mills grenade detonators in their tin

in reserve during the disastrous British gas attacks at Loos in September 1915. From January 1916 all P Helmets were dipped in hexamine – highly absorbent of phosgene gas – to become the Phenate-Hexamine or 'PH Helmet'. All were clammy, cloying and unpleasant to wear.

The PH Helmet could only stop a limited amount of gas, with the likelihood of failure if pushed to its limit by high concentrations of phosgene. In order to improve this situation, Bertram Lambert, a chemistry lecturer at Oxford, developed the concept of layers of lime and sodium permanganate to deal

with a range of gases, and this concept was to lead to the development of the 'Large Box Respirator' (LBR) in 1915–16. This used a 'box' of stacked granules of lime permanganate, pumice soaked in sodium sulphate, and charcoal. The box (actually a converted standard issue water bottle) was carried in a satchel, and was connected to an impregnated facemask with two eyepieces by a corrugated hose and metal mouthpiece. Large and bulky, it was only to be issued to Royal Engineer gas companies and soldiers in static positions, such as heavy machine gunners and artillerymen.

The No. 23 Mark II Mills grenade could be used as a rifle grenade (with a screw-in rod) or hand grenade, and was packed in multiples of twelve in boxes with a separate tin of detonators

Brassards worn by the men of the Royal Engineers Special Companies, responsible for releasing cloud gas and gas warfare. Left, officers' brassard, 56th (London) Division; right, other ranks' brassard

With the advent of gas as a weapon of war, some means of alerting the men in the frontline was necessary. From the early days, the army relied upon any number of extemporised warnings, including, typically, shell cases suspended from the trench sides, or from simple tripods near gun sites. Simple gas gongs had the advantage that the material from which they were constructed was readily available, and needed little more than the ability to suspend the gong upside down, and the provision of an appropriate piece of metal or wood to beat the gong with. Captain J.C.Dunn, Medical Officer with the Royal Welsh Fusiliers, recorded the soldiers' response to its use.

If a whiff of gas you smell,
Bang your gong like bloody hell,
On with your googly, up with your gun –
Ready to meet the bloody Hun

The 'Small Box Respirator' (SBR) was developed from its predecessor, in order to provide universal protection from a range of gases, while not being an encumbrance to free movement. Reducing the size of the box was the first step, by modifying its fill – placing the lime permanganate granules between two layers of charcoal. Other improvements were an exhalation valve (which also had a device to drain saliva), and a haversack that could be worn either slung over the shoulder or through the use of a lug and leather strap, which could be hitched up onto the chest (strap over the head) into the 'alert' position. The facemask was issued in four sizes, its number stamped on the mask and on the haversack. When it was worn, the soldier would grip the inner rubber mouthpiece between his teeth and use the integrated nose clip to ensure his breathing was through the box. When first issued in August–October 1916, the masks were individually fitted, and each soldier acclimatised by exposure (when wearing the mask) in a tear gas chamber for five minutes. This mask was to prove highly effective.

Rattles had been used by the Police in Victorian Britain before they were issued with whistles, and in 1917 the BEF was to issue them as an efficient means of gas warning. Rattles had the advantage that, if swung with sufficient vigour, they could be heard from some distance; in 1917 they were replaced by an even more efficient tool, an air-powered horn – known as a Strombos horn – the sound of which could carry for at least 20 miles.

In 1915, the Germans had pinned their hopes on gas being a breakthrough weapon. In 1916, for the British, it was the tank. Used in 'penny packets' at first, in 1917 the mass use of tanks at Cambrai was to be the cause of rejoicing, and they would be a major element of the new industrial battlefield of 1918. The tank, a British invention of 1915, was designed specifically for trench crossing, thereby puncturing the German lines. Its characteristic rhombic shape – destined to

Clockwise from left: The Phenate Hexamine (PH) gas hood, known as a tube helmet as the wearer had to clamp a tube in his mouth and breathe out through it. This mask was introduced in 1915; the PH Helmet was known as the 'goggle-eyed bugger with the tit' to the troops; simple satchels for carrying the PH Helmet

Opposite: Sentry post with gas alarms – a gas gong made from a shell case, and a gas rattle; a Small Box Respirator is at the ready

Clockwise from right: The Small Box Respirator (SBR) replaced the PH Helmet at the end of 1916; the SBR had a full mask, with a tube to be grasped in the mouth, and a clip to prevent breathing through the nose; instructions for the use of the SBR

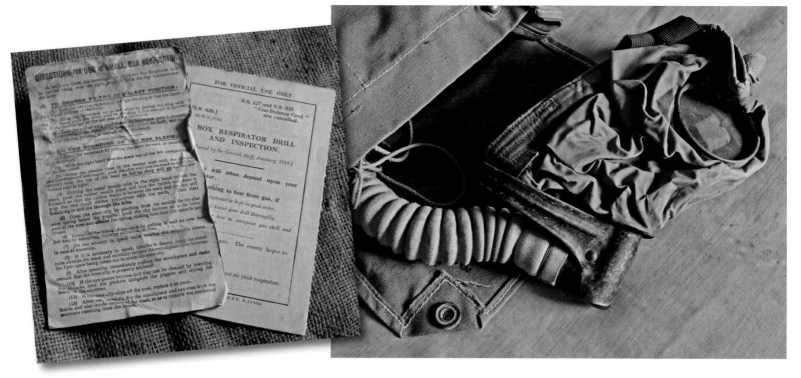

become an icon used by souvenir manufacturers, trench artists and savings schemes – was intended to give as great a surface area as possible to the tracks in order that they might both cross open trenches and climb gradients.

The Mark I was deployed for the first time on the latter stages of the Somme, the *Daily Mirror* newspaper having already carried the first pictures to be released of the tank in action. The tank was to evolve during the war, increasing its reliability, the Mark IV being the main battle tank of the later war period. It was deployed in two basic forms, with 6in guns (male) and with Lewis or Hotchkiss machine guns (female) arming their side-mounted sponsons. Both, travelling at an average speed of 4 miles per hour, would be vulnerable to shellfire. Operated by men of the Machine Gun Corps (Heavy Section) at first, by July 1917 a new corps had evolved: the Tank Corps. The use of tanks was to be decisive in the final battles of the Great War.

OVER THE BAGS

For the infantryman, going 'over the top' or 'over the bags' was, relatively speaking, a rare event. The large set-piece battles so commonly associated with the Great War took a considerable amount of planning, with extended periods of artillery preparation and the gathering of reinforcements in the rear areas, clogging transport arteries and communication trenches. Nevertheless, most infantry soldiers would experience at some point the terror of rising out of the trenches in broad daylight to face the enemy that they had previously only caught fleeting glimpses of through trench periscopes. The resulting battles have become a heated discussion point over the decades

since the end of the war. More common were trench raids at night; everything from single officers exploring no man's land, to organised miniature offensives protected by complex box barrages. Trench raids were deemed by the High Command to be an operational necessity, required for at least two reasons: to provide information on the enemy in the trenches ahead, and to maintain the offensive spirit.

Artillery was a key component of all attacks; massing guns and having sufficient ammunition to subdue the enemy became essential if an offensive was to succeed. For the British, supply of guns and ammunition took some time to catch up with the ambitions of the General Staff, and in early 1915 the inadequacy of the supply led to the fall of the Liberal Government during the 'shell crisis'. With inadequate ammunition to support the Neuve Chappelle and Fromelles offensives, the German defences were intact, the barbed wire uncut. Adequate supplies would have to await the work of the newly formed Ministry of Munitions mobilising effort on the home front. Nevertheless, the effects of pre-battle bombardments were impressive, even in 1915.

The sentry was standing up, with his elbows on the ground level (there was no parapet) gazing alert and interested at the continuous flicker of our shells bursting along the enemy's trenches. Overhead was the continual griding, screeching, whistling of the shells as they passed over, without pause or cessation; behind there was a chain of gun-flickers the other side of the ridge; and in front was another chain of flashes, and a succession of bump, bump, bumps as the shells burst relentlessly in the German trenches.

Lt B. Adams, Royal Welsh Fusiliers, 1915

But it was the Battle of the Somme, 1916, the first major British offensive on the Western Front since Loos in September 1915, which was to demonstrate the power of artillery. The bombardment of the German lines that opened on 24 June 1916 and that lasted until zero hour on 1 July 1916, became known as *Trommelfeuer*: drumfire. Intended to destroy enemy batteries, trenches, dugouts and barbed wire, the bombardment involved ceaseless shelling from almost 1,500 guns and howitzers of all types firing some 1.7 million rounds. But even this level of fire was inadequate for a front of 18 miles. The men who went over the top at 7.30 a.m., zero hour on 1 July 1916, climbed out of their trenches over the sandbag parapet to face the German survivors, who were ready to meet them.

At zero hour soldiers experienced the terror of climbing from their trenches to face the unknown. Rising from the trenches was achieved by trench ladders, more often than not duckboards with some of the slats removed. Putting these in place would remind the soldiers of their coming responsibilities. Coordinating the attack were the subalterns – junior officers in charge of platoons who would face the dangers of no man's land with their NCOs and men – often conspicuous with their Sam Browne belts and open-necked uniform. With officers in their distinctive garb more often than not targeted by the enemy, it is not surprising that some would adopt the dress of the ordinary soldier, with discrete rank badges carried on the shoulder straps of an ordinary 'Tommy's' tunic.

Equipped with whistles, wristwatches and the hefty Mark VI Webley revolver – first issued in 1915 and capable of stopping any man with its powerful .455-calibre bullet – it would be these officers who would signify the attack in the eerie silence that

Opposite: The tank. The British wonder weapon, here a Mark IV female, equipped with machine guns, in training at Hatfield, Hertfordshire

followed the end of the bombardment. It is not surprising, then, that the whistle has entered into the mythology of the war. Most were made by the famous firm of Hudson's, in Birmingham, the manufacturer of 'The Metropolitan' police whistle and its military versions since the mid part of the nineteenth century. Yet whistles were employed on other tasks, too: warning of gas attacks, for instance, or, more usually, sentries keeping watch by day through periscopes for incoming 'minnies'. As these were easily spotted in flight, sentries would blow their whistles and shout 'minnies to the left' or 'right' as appropriate.

Struggling forward over no man's land, soldiers would be pushed into a maelstrom of machine-gun fire, counter bombardment and the broken landscape of the battlefield. Overhead was the bombardment that was intended to protect the attackers, a moving curtain of shellfire that would attempt to clear the trenches in front of the living wave of men.

The battlefield would change over the course of the war, with tanks and aircraft taking their place alongside the infantryman in the coordinated, all arms attacks of 1918. Most men would find it disorienting, and getting into the enemy's trenches was

Opposite: Attacks were preceded by artillery bombardment

Left: News of Sir Douglas Haig's great offensive, July 1916

Opposite: Zero hour

Clockwise from right: Preparing to go 'over the bags', trench ladders in position; the SMLE wire cutter attachment; loading the SMLE with a charger of five rounds of .303 ammunition

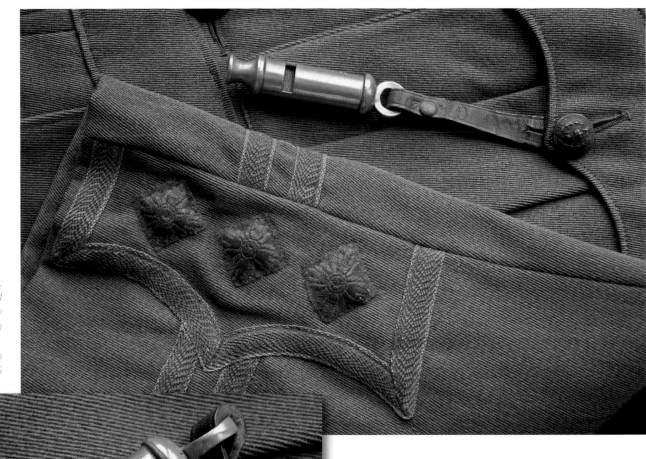

Right: Officer's whistle; this officer has disguised his rank badges by blackening them

Below: Hudson 'trench whistle', 1915

a terrifying experience. Not every attack would be a major one, however; trench raids were more often than not an important means of establishing control over the battlefront, or simply a means of gaining intelligence of who exactly was occupying the trenches opposite. Capturing prisoners who could be interrogated, or even just the gathering of insignia from dead soldiers, was deemed important to gain intelligence. Raids varied from small affairs with small groups of men, to larger ones involving artillery preparation. In all cases, grenades would be the most significant weapons, as would a variety of extemporised weapons that had close links with medieval warfare.

Raid weaponry: trench clubs and an improvised dagger, the 'French nail'

Of all the items associated with trench warfare, the rediscovery of clubs and knives as weapons is identified with the descent of warfare from the ideal of open battle to the extended and stalemated nightmare of the trenches. Of all weapons, clubs have an ancestry that extends back millennia. In the strict confines of the trench, rifles with fixed bayonets could not be wielded effectively, and where a modicum of surprise was needed, the club, knife, revolver and grenade found favour in night trench raids. In most cases, clubs and knives were fashioned from whatever was to hand – made both by soldiers themselves and in the workshops of the Army Ordnance Corps. Typical clubs had a long turned-wood handle studded with boot cleats; other examples of these have nails instead of cleats. Different versions were probably improvised in the trenches, or even at home and sent to the front.

In most cases, the standard British 1907 pattern bayonet was too long to be of any effective use in trench raids. As no official knives were to be issued to British troops, homemade examples were actively employed. It has been suggested that the knife was not a preferred weapon on British trench raids; using a bayonet on the end of rifle as trained was one thing, but getting close enough to stab a man with a knife was another. While other nations were issued with short knives for battle use, the British soldier resorted to privately purchased examples, or to manufacturing their own close to the frontline. Typical of this industry was the use of cut-down bayonets – the Canadian Ross bayonet (for the ill-fated Ross Rifle, withdrawn as being unfit for frontline service in late 1916), already relatively short, was a favourite, but any other suitable piece of metal that would carry a blade was also pressed into service.

The aftermath of an attack would be the suffering of men, many of whom would be stranded in no man's land, sheltering in shell holes. In the Great War, the rate and scale of casualties is still breath-taking: infamously, the opening hour of the Battle of the Somme on 1 July 1916 saw at least 50,000 men killed, wounded or reported missing. Some 10–15 per cent of soldiers mobilised were killed, but many more were wounded or taken prisoner, and it was relatively rare for a frontline soldier to survive the war completely unscathed. Wounding was a common experience; most longed for the opportunity of gaining a minor wound that would take them back home to Blighty. Not everyone would have the opportunity.

Dear Kitty
Just a few line hoping you are alright I am in hospital and as you will see by the writing that I am not a very good position. I am waiting to come across to Blighty. Tell Jack that he was very lucky not to come across here.

Pte Percy Edwards, 17th Battalion, Royal Welsh Fusiliers, 23 September 1918 (died of wounds, 83rd General Hospital, Boulogne, 28 September 1918)

Stretcher-bearers were battalion men who gave up their arms to carry their stretcher, the bearing of arms by medics being expressly forbidden in war. Ideally, at least six men would be needed per stretcher; this was not always achievable, and German prisoners were often drafted in to carry wounded soldiers back, as it was an offence under king's regulations to escort wounded soldiers back without the express permission of an officer. Regimental stretcher-bearers wore

Opposite: Prisoner taken in the Battle of the Somme, 13 July 1916

*Right: Regimental
stretcher-bearer's brassard*

*Below: Regimental
stretcher-bearer serving
with the Queen's
Westminster Rifles
(16th London Regiment)*

a brassard or armband bearing the initials 'SB'. Many were bandsmen, others were infantrymen detailed for the job – a dangerous task, requiring service under fire, usually in no man's land.

Nobody moved about in daylight with impunity. Stretcher-bearers … crossed shell-swept 'No Man's Land' on their errand of mercy, and always the enemy fired upon them. Shots followed them from start to finish, and for coldly calculated bravery their persistence was hard to beat, even in a war teaming with heroism.

Pte Arthur E. Lambert, 2nd Battalion, Honourable Artillery Company

Regimental stretcher-bearers' responsibilities ended at the regimental aid post; from here men would be dispatched to the rear areas and would be in the care of the Royal Army Medical Corps (RAMC). These men wore the red Geneva Cross armbands and the trade badge of the medical orderly – again a red Geneva Cross – and their role was (as part of the Army Medical Services) to care for the wounded and to evacuate them efficiently from the frontline. Movement from the front was long, laborious and, for the wounded, painful. The chain was a long one: first to the Regimental Aid Post (RAP), run by an RAMC doctor and small number of orderlies, which was set up close to the frontline and adjacent to battalion headquarters (usually in dugouts or ruined buildings). Next in the chain was the Advanced Dressing Station (ADS), set up at the farthest front-wards limit of wheeled transport, and run by the RAMC Field Ambulance, with three such units of men attached to an infantry division.

I had only once looked into the dressing station, although I must have passed it several hundred times. I was surprised at its size: there were two compartments. As I stepped down inside, I wondered whether it was shell-proof.

Lt B. Adams, Royal Welsh Fusiliers, 1915

At the dressing stations, attention was given to saving the lives of badly wounded men, and to stabilising their condition before they could be passed on down the chain. The wounded would then be transported from an RAP to an ADS through a variety of means: on foot, by cart, on a stretcher – the latter with a series of relay posts, as there was a considerable distance between the two. Men could then expect to be transported down the line to the Main Dressing Station (MDS), beyond the range of medium artillery fire; the Casualty Clearing Station (CCS), set up beyond the artillery zone; and finally, still within the theatre of operations, General and Stationary hospitals. From here, Tommy would hope to receive his 'ticket' – a label that marked him for transportation on hospital ships bound for Blighty.

After the surgeon dressed my arm, I said, 'Is there any chance of this getting me to Blighty?' And I thought he did not hear; he was looking the other way. But suddenly I heard that calm deliberate voice: 'Yes, that is a Blighty one.'

Lt B. Adams, Royal Welsh Fusiliers, 1915

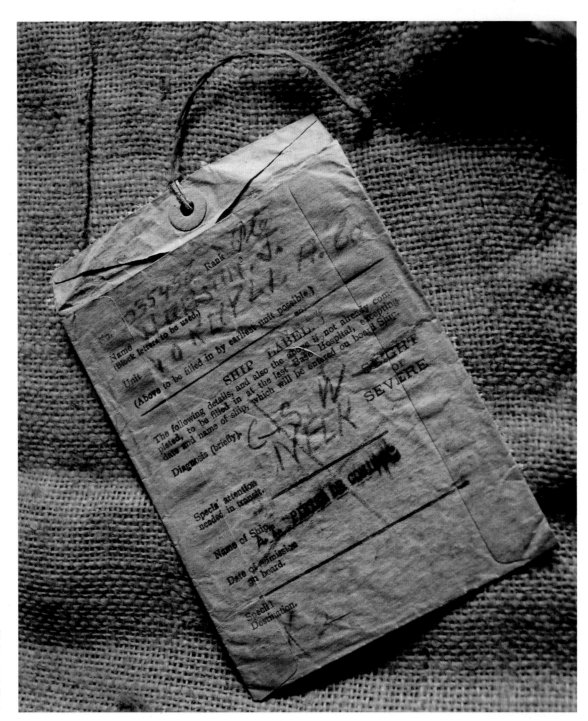

Casualty label that would be tied to a wounded soldier: Private Hobson survived this wound to the neck, but was killed later in the war

With the wounded retrieved in the aftermath of battle, there was another important task, searching the battlefield for bodies. As this often had to wait some time, it was frequently a grisly job.

There were many other bodies lying out in this shell-churned area and the ghastly stench of mangled corpses gripped us all as we carried out our task. It was very sad, but the headless and armless go exactly the same treatment. We searched all for their identity discs, and their Army Books 64, and any other personal belongings for their next of kin.

Capt. F.C. Hitchcock, Leinster Regiment, 1915

A soldier's effects

CHURCH ARMY
OPEN TO ALL

PASSED BY CENSOR

Miss K. Tommy
20 AUG 18
Argoed, Hall
Llangollen

28-9-18

General Hospital
Boulogne
France

Dear Kitty
        just a line hoping you are
...ight I am in hospital and as you will see by
...writing that I am not a very good position...
...am waiting to came across to Blighty...
...Jack that he was very lucky no...
...come across here you asked whether
...a letter from him I have not received
...from him since he was at Limme...
...I will close with best love
...ed with a loving
kiss   yours truly

19/18
Dear Kitty I have
...the line and...
...to the ba...

Identification of the dead was essential if families were to be given the news of the death of their loved ones, and graves registration was the responsibility of the army in the field. Soldiers found were buried, their details recorded and passed back to the War Office for transmission to the next of kin. Very often, people would be waiting anxiously to hear whether their loved ones had made it through.

We are waiting & longing to hear of Jake. This is the 6th week since we heard from him that was just before he went into the battle at Aubers Rdge. He is in hospital in France & that is all we can discover, which news we had through a lady who has influence at the War Office. I believe that no official news has reached home yet of any kind. Practically the whole of his battalion was wiped out.

Letter dated 14 June 1915

Receiving a telegram or other notification from the War Office was dreaded by all at home during the war; more often than not it would signify that a loved one had been killed, wounded or taken prisoner. In other households, the first inklings of a casualty might be a letter returned home with the brutal and stark message 'Killed in Action' written or stamped as a cachet on its unopened cover; in other cases, letters would be written from the adjutant or chaplain to soften the blow. More often than not, these letters would profess that the soldier in question had not suffered, and had died instantly; the truth might be harder to bear. In the case of Private Charles Chard of Somerset, serving with the Yorkshire Regiment, the colonel of his battalion was to write, 'Pte Chard was killed in the Arras Sector in August 1917 while out on a daylight patrol instantaneously, he is buried in the Sunken Road Cemetery in Fampoux.'

Soldiers' comrades also took it upon themselves to write to their friends' families, who must have found some comfort in their words. Following the death of Private Herbert Dando in the Battle of Arras, on 23 April 1917, his friend Private Steeter took time to write to Mrs Dando.

Dear Mrs Dando,
Just a line to you expressing my Deepest Sympathy on behalf of your Dear Husband which lost his life while fighting for his Country. I can honestly say that he died a hero and I feel the loss of him very much for we were brothers together ever since we left England. I myself has [sic] been wounded but going on well and may God help you and keep you. Bert was killed on April 23rd.

A. Steeter, 1st Battalion, The Queen's, France

Private Dando has no known grave; one of countless thousands who are commemorated on memorials to the missing that dot the landscape of France and Flanders.

Opposite: Families often heard of the death of their loved ones by returned letters; these are from Private Percy Edwards, Royal Welsh Fusiliers, died of wounds on 28 September 1918

OUT OF THE LINE

It is a strange place, this belt of land behind the firing-line. The men are out of the trenches for three days, and then it is their duty, after perhaps a running parade before breakfast and two or three hours' drill and inspection in the morning, to rest for the remainder of the day.

Lt B. Adams, Royal Welsh Fusiliers, 1915

If 'up the line' meant a spell in the frontline trenches, 'out on rest' could mean a great many different things, depending on the sector, the army or divisional commander, or the exigencies of battle. For most soldiers, a spell in the frontline meant time spent in very present and imminent danger: shellfire, random bullets, gas, the morning 'hate' – all could spell immediate and random death and wounding. Away from the trenches, Tommy could resume some connection with normality, a release of tension, and an opportunity to forget, particularly when the strains of frontline life started to tell.

Life in the trenches we all loathe, and no one makes any bones about it or pretends to like it – except for a few rare exciting minutes, which are very few and far between. But then you come into billets, and recover; and so you can carry on.

Lt B. Adams, Royal Welsh Fusiliers, 1915

After a tour of duty in the frontline, on average seven days, a battalion would be relieved. Its destination would be the reserve trenches – duty less prone to sniping and trench mortars, but still subject to the random vagaries of artillery fire.

Men in reserve could be called upon to reinforce the front when under pressure, and would be the main stock of reinforcements when the front was under severe pressure.

Dear Sister. Just a few lines to let you know that I am still alive and in the best of health but I have had a bit of skin shot off the end of my thumb. I only came out of the trenches last night after 48 hours. I have been in a good many times now.

Pte W. Astbury, 5th Battalion Cheshire Regiment, France

They would also be called upon to supply the frontline, to carry equipment, rations and numerous other items into the trenches they had so recently vacated.

More welcome was the withdrawal of a battalion out of the line completely, relieving it from trench duty. This was a means of gaining some rest, a chance for officers and NCOs to reassert military fastidiousness, and an opportunity for the average soldier to gain some mental freedom – washing, speaking to locals, buying trinkets. Depending on the theatre of war, they could be based in villages, set up in hutted or tented camps, or simply organised

Three men from the trenches, pictured in France. Obviously battle-hardened veterans from the Essex Regiment, the man in the centre wears a wounded stripe and a Military Medal ribbon

in the least dangerous (a relative term) part of the battle zone. Soldiers would return, wet, weary and verminous, but glad to be in a position outside the immediate firing line.

Here we are back in billets at last. We are a disreputable gang of ruffians when we march back, even after six dry days. The men all have their goatskin coats on, or what remains of them, but they have so many straps and things to carry that you only see tufs of hair sticking out hear [sic] and there. Some of them have braziers, bags of coke, waterproof sheets, and all varieties of

woolly caps, and the most amazing styles of lower garments that you could ever imagine, for to keep their legs warm, in spite of the kilt, they have set to work with sacking and canvas.

Lt A.D. Gillespie, Argyll and Sutherland Highlanders, March 1915

Soldiers out on rest were housed in a variety of billets. In France and Flanders, this could be a battered village, showing the scars of long-range shelling or the movement of armies in the early days of the war. In the aftermath of a retirement, the Germans

Visé Paris 800

Sketches of Tommy's life
Out on rest – N° 7   It looks rather pretty to see a picture of us at dinner in the yard of one of our billets, doesn't it?

F. Mackain

Billets were a major change from the trenches

often laid waste to the country, ensuring that any rest would be uncomfortable.

I have had a wash and shave and am feeling fine. Fritz does not leave us any decent billets he blows everything up before he leaves it and he has even cut down the trees in this part of the country.

Pte Herbert Dando, The Queen's (Royal West Surrey Regiment), April 1917

In all cases, competition for the best billets was intense, especially if another battalion had got there first. When they were billeted upon people grimly holding on to their existence, barns stuffed with bunks, haylofts and outbuildings all formed ways of accommodating the men; in other cases, taking up residence in farmhouses, sharing the kitchen with the still-resident family was a possibility.

There is not much elegance about our billet; this room has a bare floor, bare walls except for a hideous frieze of grapes and vine-leaves painted around the top, and a mirror, damp and blurred, with a line where someone has drawn on it with his fingers; then over the mantel-piece, or rather the stove, is a case of everlasting flowers, and two gilt china jugs, which can only have escaped breaking by a miracle … But it's a nice cheerful place compared with the trenches.

Lt A.D. Gillespie, Argyll and Sutherland Highlanders, 1915

Rest camps were also set up in rear areas, though often still within range of the largest guns. These could be in tented accommodation, though more weather-proof hutted camps were another option – these huts at least provided reasonably dry and secure accommodation. Nissen Huts, developed in 1916 and made from arched, corrugated steel sections, were also an option.

We were relieved and went back to Canada Huts for a rest of four days. Oh, that first rest out of the trenches! The accommodation was poor enough seen in the light of home comforts, but what a palace of rest and refreshment it seemed to me then, and how quickly the time passed.

Lt Francis Buckley, 7th Battalion, Northumberland Fusiliers

In all cases, on-rest soldiers could once more feel human; here shedding the dirty, lice-ridden wet clothing of the trenches was of utmost importance. To this end, the army organised bathhouses in the rear areas (run by the ever-present Army Service Corps) that provided the means of ridding both bodies and uniforms of lice. Often organised in breweries, baths were set up wherever there was the possibility of furnishing vats of hot water through which men moved in a constant stream – while their uniforms were baked in ovens in an attempt to kill both lice and their eggs. Issued with clean underwear, for a short time the men could attempt to stay really clean; but all too often they became re-infested with vermin in billets.

Being in billets and out on rest meant an escape from the tension of frontline life. This was the opportunity to try out the local language – hopelessly mangled and mixed with words from the Indian Empire – and to receive and spend the local currency that would be issued while on rest. In many cases, they could mix with civilians – those brave or foolish enough to be close to the battle zone – talking in strange, anglicised versions of the prevailing language with their hosts. They could also engage women in hopeful conversations, although most who remained close to the frontline were long past an age where this hope would bear fruit.

Women were working, or gossiping at the doorsteps. The estaminet {café} doors were flung wide open, and the floors were being scrubbed and sprinkled with sawdust. A little bare-legged girl, in a black cotton dress, was hugging a great white loaf; an old man sat blinking in the sunshine; cats were basking, dogs nosing about lazily.

Lt B. Adams, Royal Welsh Fusiliers, 1915

Soldiers were paid in the local currency, and their buying power could be put to work in the purchase of alcohol – often of lamentable quality – and to indulge in other vices normally frowned upon at home: gambling, fraternisation with women of 'ill repute', even visits to brothels, the so-called 'red lamps'. Along the battle zone, *estaminets* sprang up in cottages, farmhouses and other village buildings as the locals more

Estaminets sprung up in cottages, selling café-au-lait and vin ordinaire

Sketches
of Tommy's life
Out on rest – Nº 5

A regular carouse of coffee and fried eggs is one of the things we always have when we get to one of these villages.

Visé Paris 800

often than not saw the opportunity to make some money from their guests. *Café-au-lait*, weak beer, *vin ordinaire* and *oeuf-frites* were provided en masse for the British soldier.

Gambling too was a draw, and the traditional games of peacetime soldiery would be available to take money away from the gullible. Gambling has always been a part of army life, and the opportunity to engage in this 'sport', especially when Tommy had money in his pocket, saw the establishment of a large number of illegal gambling schools – particularly engaged in 'Crown and Anchor'. Crown and Anchor is a traditional gambling game of the British Navy, using

a canvas board and scrimshaw dice. Spread throughout the services, it was also usually seen as 'a mug's game', with the banker, who owned the board – usually a much-folded and battered specimen – as the likely winner.

Private Stephen Graham of the Scots Guards described the game being played in the manner of his forefathers before Waterloo, with huddled masses of soldiery gathered around the 'boards', traditionally divided into six sections, each marked with a symbol: heart, crown, diamond, spade, anchor and club. Three special dice have the same symbols on their faces – and the gamble was to place money on the board

Crown and Anchor

Housey-Housey was a tamer pursuit than the rough and tumble of Crown and Anchor

Sketches of Tommy's life At the Base. — N° 3

" House " is the most popular game at the Base. Who hasn't heard those familiar lines : « Eyes down ! Legs eleven ! Kelly's eye Blind half hundred ! And another lucky old dip in the bag ! ».

predicting the likely outcome. Money placed on the winning symbols was doubled up, but more often than not would be lost to the banker. As with other games, the symbols would have their own nicknames, recorded by Graham: the crown – the sergeant major; the spade – the shovel; the diamond – the curse; the anchor – the meat-hook. Crown and Anchor being strictly frowned upon by the army, 'Housey-Housey' (bingo) was the only officially sanctioned game; there were nevertheless plenty of punters to be found for harder gambling pursuits.

A shilling a day, minus stoppages and plus allowances for proficiency of up to sixpence, was all the average

Opposite: Soldiers were paid in the local currency while in France

British soldier could expect in his pay packet – at least until pay was revised in 1917. The officer-only Army Pay Department, and its corps of clerks, the Army Pay Corps, handled accountancy in the army – a rather unglamorous, but nevertheless essential job – keeping records of the issue of money to the troops at home and abroad. In theatre, issue of pay to the soldiery was made by its own officers, drawn from divisional field cashiers, the issue of pay duly noted in the individual soldier's pay book (AB64). In France, the prevailing exchange rate was in the order of 25 francs to the pound; the pound being worth 20 shillings. The average rate of pay per week was 10 francs, minus any stoppages.

I have just 'paid out' — all in five and twenty-franc notes. 'In the field' every man has his own pay book which the officer must sign, while the company quartermaster-sergeant sees that his acquittance roll is also signed by Tommy. We had a small table and chair out in the yard, and in an atmosphere of pigs and poultry I dealt out the blue and white oblongs which have already in many cases been converted into bread. For that is where most of the pay money goes, there and in the estaminets.

Lt B. Adams, Royal Welsh Fusiliers, 1915

The most frequently encountered note was the convenient 10-franc version, together with the usual 2-franc and 1-franc silver coins, and numerous centimes, which must have cluttered Tommy's pockets after a night spent in an *estaminet* drinking *vin blanc* and weak beer, and eating egg and chips. Tommy would also have some freedom to make simple purchases, such souvenirs as there were, including silk postcards and other trinkets from those civilians brave enough to remain.

I am sending you a silk card with this letter which I promised you some time ago, but have only just had time to get one, and hope you will get it safe, I will also send your mother one as soon as I can because I know that she would prize it.

Pte Ted Barnes, Devonshire Regiment,
June 1917

Silk postcards were produced early on in 1915 as the locals realised the potential for the marketing of their skills; some estimates suggest that as many as 10 million cards were produced during the war — all handmade. Each card was produced as part of a cottage industry,

Opposite: Favoured souvenirs: the German Pickelhaube helmet and iron cross

which saw mostly women engaged in hand embroidering intricate designs on to strips of silk mesh, the design being repeated as many as twenty-five times on a strip, before being sent to a factory for cutting and mounting as postcards and greetings cards. There was a huge range. Rifleman Dennis and his fellow soldiers of the 21st KRRC were attracted by their sentimental messages — 'friendship', 'birthday greetings', 'Home Sweet Home' and so on were popular — it was a chance to send their wishes home 'from the trenches'.

Tommy was an inveterate souvenir hunter; many battle souvenirs would be parcelled off home or carried back when Tommy went on leave. In his classic *Twelve Days on the Somme*, Sydney Rogerson of the West Yorkshire Regiment describes the lengths that members of his battalion went to gather objects that could be sold on to the 'base-wallahs' and non-frontline troops — enough to fund the desire for extra Woodbines, cheap *vin rouge* and thin beer when out on rest. The 'flotsam of battle' was collected — shell nose caps, grenades, German cap rosettes, weapons, gloves and boots, as well as the highly prized hardy perennial, the *Pickelhaube*. Officers and men alike were not immune to the collecting craze.

We took it in shifts with my heavy bags of souvenirs. One package had four 'Little Willie' cases inside, in other words, the cast iron shell cases ... The haversack was filled with aluminium fuse tops and one large piece of a 'Jack Johnson' shell case. My pockets — and I had a good number, as I was wearing my greatcoat — were filled with a variety of objects.

Capt. Bruce Bairnsfather, Royal Warwickshire Regiment, 1915

*Above: Fragments of the
ruined towns were picked
up as souvenirs. Ypres, so
close to the frontline, was
razed to the ground over
the course of the war*

*Right: Stained glass from
the ruined St Martin's
Cathedral, Ypres: a
soldier's souvenir*

Other prized uniform articles were the German belt plate – with its distinctive message *Gott mit Uns* – and medals: items all too easily removed from prisoners.

What all the men were after really was the Iron Cross, the dream of every souvenir-hunter, and which, were the lucky finder mercenary enough too wish to dispose of it, commanded a very good market.

Lt Sidney Rogerson,
West Yorkshire Regiment, 1916

Undoubtedly, this passion for collectables put the men at risk, if only – as with Bairnsfather's classic cartoon, 'Give it a good 'ard 'un Bert' – from overzealous extraction of brass nose caps from all-too-common 'duds'. Usually, nose caps were plentiful – shrapnel shell fuses were blown off easily to release the balls within – and not only from enemy shells, but also from friendly fire falling short. As described by Private Patrick McGill of the London Irish Rifles in 1915, local civilians also set up shop to sell the 'percussion cap of the death-dealing shell for half a franc'.

Some souvenirs could be transformed into 'trench art', folk art of the war, reusing the bullets, shell cases, copper drive bands, fragments of aircraft, pieces of wood and other detritus of war. Trench art was sometimes made by soldiers in the frontline, but more often manufactured in the rear areas where there was more access to tools and equipment. Typical soldier items include decorated shell cases, letter openers, matchbox folds, lighters, tanks and field caps.

Most men wanted some respite from the strictures of army life whilst on rest, and *estaminets* certainly provided an opportunity for more boisterous entertainment, but as always there was the YMCA and other charitable organisations, such as the Church Army, providing huts that allowed soldiers to gather as they had done at the training camps in 1914. Present in rest camps, and under the sign of 'Tommy's triangle', the YMCA also operated in quite advanced areas, offering some comforts to the troops.

We had a YMCA hut close to the camp, and it was interesting to drop in and have a chat with the men in charge and a cup of cocoa. There was an old gentleman there, in command, who was rightly proud of being the civilian nearest to the front line. He displayed to us with great pride a souvenir found in Ypres, the huge base of a 17-inch shell – it was almost too heavy for one man to lift. We had our Church Service and our concerts in the marquee attached to the YMCA hut.

Lt Francis Buckley, 7th Battalion,
Northumberland Fusiliers

These huts provided a means for men to gather, drink tea, eat sandwiches and write letters home on the paper provided; to kill time before their return to the trenches, and in between the military duties that still persisted while 'out on rest'. Provision of writing paper, envelopes and cards was a particularly important aspect of hut life, funded by the public's enthusiasm for flag days and street collections at home. However, devoid of alcohol, the huts were not always as welcome as they could be.

Arras was a deserted town, no egg and chips, no wine, just army canteens, YMCA and Church Army huts in which to spend our pay; how we missed the French estaminets of Flanders.

Pte Groom, London Rifle Brigade

In addition to the huts provided by charitable organisations, there were the Expeditionary Force Canteens (EFC), mostly organised and run by the Army Service Corps. They also provided a means of purchasing necessaries: paper, pencils, food and sauces that would make the ubiquitous bully beef of the trenches more palatable. Finally, 'Toc H' – from signallers' phonetic spelling of TH, or Talbot House, in Poperinge – still surviving today, provides an example of the various soldiers' respites that were set up by industrious individuals, in this case Reverend 'Tubby' Clayton, who welcomed all-comers and invited them to 'abandon all rank ye who enter here'.

In order to keep Tommy's mind off gambling, drinking and other vices, and to maintain morale in general, it was understood at a very early stage that the provision of suitable entertainments would be a benefit. There is no doubt that for men starved of

Opposite: Trench art: punching a regimental badge on a German shell case

Left: The soft chalk of Artois and Picardy was suitable for carving into regimental badges, like this, of a South Staffordshire Regiment soldier

entertainment, and particularly entertainment that might involve women, this form of release would be valuable. As early as 1914, concert parties were being created by those servicemen with a theatrical bent, and the concept was to spread so that every theatre of war, and almost every major unit of the British Army, had its own brand of concert party. Others were laid on by charitable organisations, like the ubiquitous YMCA. Often, these were associated with divisions, such as the Pierrot troupe – 'the Acorns' of the 40th Division, whose distinctive insignia was a bantam cock and acorn – which entertained the soldiers of the division at rest. The Pierrot format has a long tradition in comic theatre, and although strange to today's eyes, with the dress of ruff, white outfit and black buttons, it would have signified a good turn on the Great War stage.

Londoner Frederick Walker, enlisted under the Derby Scheme in 1916, and destined to be gassed before the end of the war, was a keen amateur music hall artiste. Singing comic songs, he would provide welcome entertainment alongside his fellow acorns, very typical of the day. Female roles would be convincingly played by young slim men, and soldiers could forget they were fellow combatants. In some rare cases, French girls could be drafted in to provide a feminine flavour – as with the celebrated pair from Armentières, 'Glycerine and Vaseline', who were to see action in many a concert party in the area.

At the time of the Great War, cinema was the new popular medium of entertainment. It didn't take long before the army cottoned on to the value of cinema in maintaining morale – and the hardworking and ubiquitous Army Service Corps was detailed to provide and run the machinery. The showing of comedy shorts – especially those of Charlie Chaplin – and Western films were particularly well received.

Opposite: YMCA worker. As at home, the YMCA provided respite from army life close to the frontline

Left: The supply of YMCA stationery was important to soldiers writing home while on rest

For the average soldier on the Western Front, leave would come only rarely – once a year if he was lucky – with officers having leave more frequently – granted at around four months. Detailed direct from the frontline, the men would have to find their way back on the long, laborious trail home – and if home was in the more remote corners of the British Isles, this could be a trek indeed. Issued with a warrant to travel, those in France and Flanders were at least able to get to Blighty in relatively short order.

Many thanks for your last letter ... received on my return from 10 days leave. I had exactly a week at home and a day in London at each end where I met numerous pals & spent 2 very good evenings there.

Pte A.E. Ferguson, France, 21 August 1917

Getting home would require considerable skill and determination, as well as the necessary paperwork. Leave could also be a frustrating experience for those

Opposite: Familiar brands could be bought at the Expeditionary Force Canteen, a means of making army food palatable

Below: Royal Field Artillery concert party. A large number of these Pierrot troupes existed

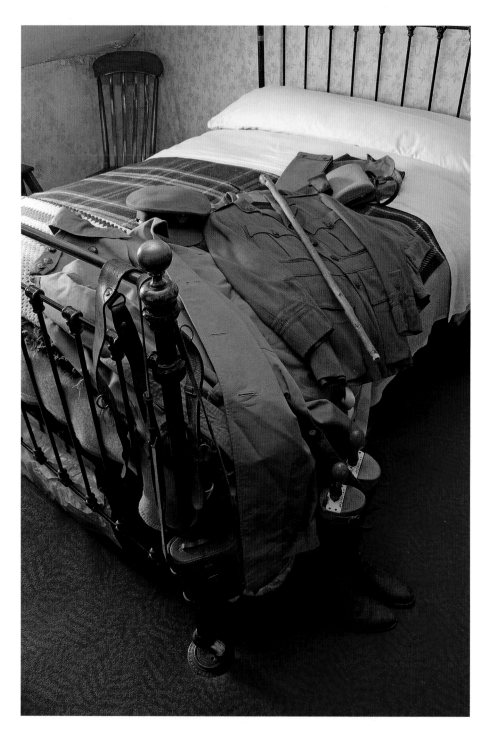

based at the remote corners of the British Isles, as the journey would be long and arduous, and it was common for the soldier to return home in full kit with the mud of Flanders still on his uniform. Not every soldier found it an easy experience; the ignorance of frontline conditions by the general populace being an oft-quoted phenomenon.

With the general paucity of home leave, letters to and from the front were of the greatest importance in maintaining the morale. For the soldiers themselves, it was sufficient to write 'On Active Service' on the card or envelope, and the letter would be posted, carrying the postmark or cachet of the army field post office. Each letter was opened by the relevant officer, who appended his signature to say that he had read its contents and had struck through any offending passages with a blue pencil. Typical 'offences' were references to current locations, defences, offensives or casualties. A further random check could be made once the letter was in transit. In response, letter writers would go to great lengths to set up a code system, perhaps using capital letters of consecutive sentences to spell out a place. More innocently, letters from home might have stamps placed in odd positions to indicate love or other personal messages.

Stationery used by the troops was provided from many sources: bought locally in shops in the base or rear areas, supplied from home, obtained from the many YMCA and Church Army huts, or gathered from 'comforts funds' set up at home. Manufacturers were not slow to catch on, and provided special sets of envelopes and paper. For most soldiers, the preferred means of writing their letters was the ubiquitous copy ink pencil; although much promoted by companies like Swan, the fountain pen was just too impractical under service conditions.

Parcels from home were essential to the troops; they provided an opportunity for families to supply the soldiers with comforts and food; balaclava helmets, cigarettes, cakes, socks, soap, candles and a host of other useful objects were requested and sent out to the front.

Dear Auntie Esther. I take this opportunity [to] thank you for the splendid parcel which I received a few days ago. I enjoyed the cake and mince pies and also the tobacco. The soap and shaving soap will come in very useful. I cannot thank you enough for your kindness.

Pte R.G. Evans, Royal Welsh Fusiliers,
1 January 1917

These parcels might well be received in the frontline, or while the soldier was out on rest. When soldiers had been killed in action or died of wounds, it was common practice for men to share their fallen comrades' parcels around – and this was the usual wish of the dead soldiers' families.

The Army Postal Section of the Royal Engineers was in charge of ensuring that letters reached home safely, and it was also their job to ensure that letters and parcels arriving for the troops were delivered – often a difficult task given the movement of troops to and from the trenches, in many different action fronts. The Royal Engineers (RE) postal service was set up in 1913, with an initial establishment of ten officers and 290 other ranks intended to support an Expeditionary Force of just six divisions – it was quickly to expand. Mail for the BEF from the United Kingdom was collected by the Post Office and sent to France, gathering at Le Havre, where the RE took over. The main unit was the Field Post Office (FPO), each FPO having its own number and special cachet mark – of which there was a bewildering array. Although the FPO was little more than an iron box and flag of office, it was to provide an essential service for the men of the BEF, MEF and other overseas forces throughout the war.

While out on rest, all too often soldiers were sent back into the battle zone in order to supply the trenches with barbed wire, ammunitions or rations. Most soldiers believed that the army had something against the concept of 'resting'. At the very least, rest also meant the opportunity for the army to reimpose military standards of cleanliness, the 'bulling' of brasses and making good the equipment lost during the tour of the trenches. Men would be charged with the loss of uniform items and equipment even if this had happened under the most trying circumstances in the frontline. This would rankle with most.

'Two hours pack drill, and pay for a new handle,' I said. 'Right-Turn!' said the sergeant-major. 'Right–Wheel–Quick–March! Get your equipment on and join your platoon at once.' This last sentence was spoken in a quick undertone, as the prisoner stepped out of the door into the road. I was filling up the column headed 'Punishment awarded' on a buff-coloured Army Form, to which I appended my signature. The case just dealt with was a very dull and commonplace one, a man having 'lost' his entrenching tool handle. Most of these losses occurred in the trenches, and were dealt with the first morning in billets at company orderly-room.

Lt B. Adams, Royal Welsh Fusiliers, 1915

One of the biggest chores 'on rest' was the upkeep of the 'soldier's best friend'; it was mandatory to keep the rifle clean. This was not just part of the military

Opposite: On leave: an officer prepares his uniform for the journey back to the front

obsession with 'bull', it was essential if the principal weapon was to be effective and not jam when needed most. As such, in and out of the trenches, rifles would be subject to inspection, with the breech and barrel examined carefully for any sign of dirt that could render a weapon unserviceable, with a round jammed irretrievably in the barrel. In order to clean their rifles, each soldier was provided with 4in-wide flannel strips marked out in 2in portions

– 'four-be-two' in the language of the day – which would be passed through the barrel with the aid of a brass-tipped, and therefore weighted, cord known as a 'pull-through'. To lubricate this action a brass bottle of machine oil was provided, stored, along with the pull-through, in the butt of the rifle itself. Keeping one's rifle clean under trench conditions could be a trying task; ensuring it met with military standards in the rest camps was little better.

Opposite: Parcels were well received at the front. They contained a variety of goods: soaps, socks, foodstuffs and tobacco

Below: While on rest, a soldier could spend his time shedding the dirt of the trenches

Sketches of Tommy's life
Out on rest — N° 6

It does not take long to construct a dainty little « boudoir » for performing one's toilet.

F. Mackain

Visé Paris 800

Above: Cleaning muddy boots took some time

Right: Muddy boots: military fastidiousness returned while on rest

With the nature of trench warfare constantly changing, it was essential that men received lectures on new tactics, weapons or equipment while out on rest; here officers and men alike could assimilate the most up-to-date views on trench warfare.

Half were engaged in arm-drill under my best drill-sergeant; the other half were doing musketry in gas-helmets, an unpleasant practice which nothing could induce me to do on a sunny May morning. They lay on their fronts, legs well apart, and were working the bolts of their rifles fifteen times a minute.

Lt B. Adams, Royal Welsh Fusiliers, 1915

Above: Repairs to uniforms were often necessary after a tour of the trenches

Left: Buttons and other brasses would be polished on rest, though usually allowed to dull in the trenches

Aftermath of battle: a Military Cross ribbon is sewn on to an officer's tunic

Opposite, clockwise from bottom left: Removing the bolt and using a weighted pull-through, a piece of four-be-two, and plenty of oil; cleaning a 'soldier's best friend'; the SMLE Number III Rifle; the SMLE magazine could hold ten .303 Mark VII bullets; bullets were loaded from a charger system*

With leave so infrequent, it is not surprising that the ordinary soldier secretly wished for a simple wound or debilitating illness that would take him out of the cursed foreign land in which he was serving, back to the green fields of England. Such wounds became known as Blighty or 'cushy' wounds; sufficiently serious to be sent home on a hospital ship, slight enough not to be life threatening or debilitating. The casualty figures for the First World War are astounding. The British Empire fielded almost 9.5 million men; of those, almost a million were to lose their lives, while a further 2.1 million were to be wounded. Getting a 'Blighty wound' was dreamed of by most soldiers.

Oh if only this awful business would only come to an end! There were some who were lucky enough to get wounded with a chance of going to Blighty, but I suppose I must think myself fortunate in coming through whole.

Pte Tom Arnold, France, 1917

War hospitals up and down the country were to receive soldiers 'From the Front'. These were set up in large private houses and municipal buildings in order to satisfy the demand for suitable accommodation, and were often staffed by 'VADs', volunteer nurses

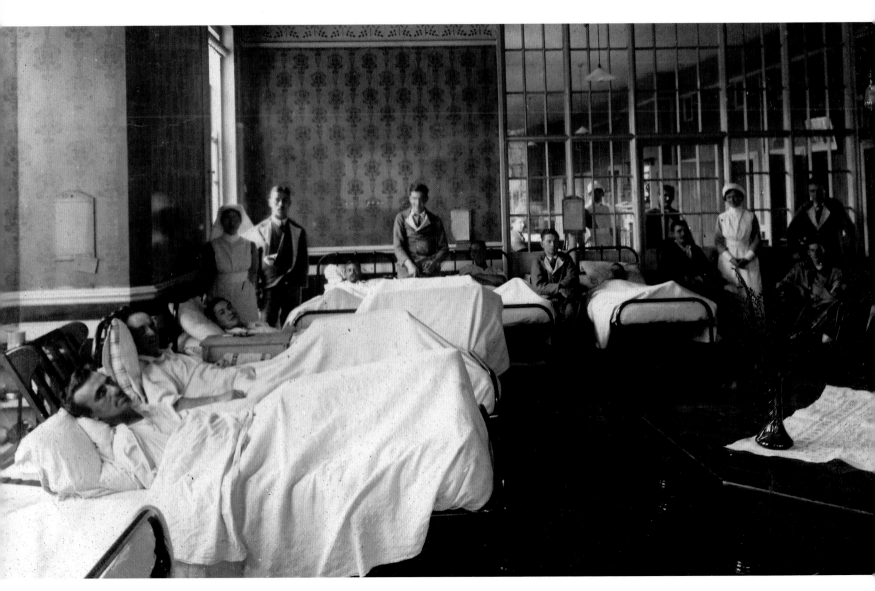

A hospital ward with
wounded soldiers

belonging to the Voluntary Aid Detachment. The VAD was set up under the auspices of the Territorial Associations in 1909, and was run by the British Red Cross Society and the Order of St John of Jerusalem in order to provide a means for women – mostly, at first, from more affluent classes – to give service in hospitals at home. With the requirements of wartime, the VAD would recruit from a much broader cross-section of society. After a short course of instruction, VAD nurses would serve alongside qualified nurses – sometimes with inevitable tension. VADs would staff all war hospitals, alongside the military nurses and RAMC personnel who made up the Army Medical Service, and some would even use their influence to be sent overseas, assisting as nurses or orderlies in hospitals in all the major theatres of war.

No. 3 General Hopital, at Le Tréport, France. Based in a once grand hotel, this Base Hopital could accommodate up to 10,000 wounded men

In both world wars, ordinary soldiers sent to hospital, and in convalescence, were ordered out of their familiar khaki and into hospital blue, a simple suit of blue clothes worn with a distinctive red tie, together with the khaki Service Dress cap, glengarry or bonnet. Cheaply produced, the blue uniform was usually lined in white, so that when worn open the lapels would contrast with the bright blue of the jacket. As the trousers were universally long, they were worn rolled up. In general, 'hospital blues' would provide a poor fit, and so officers were allowed more freedom to dress as they wished on convalescence. Soldiers wore blues as long as they were in hospital, or convalescing. At the end of their treatment, soldiers were sent to medical boards staffed by doctors, in order to assess their classification. Many would be sent back, graded A1, fit; others were downgraded in classification and sent to the Labour Corps; some, discharged. All were entitled to 'wounded stripes' for the left sleeve of their uniforms, a visible record of their experiences.

All too quickly, the period of rest would come to an end, and soldiers would have to make the journey back to the frontline and the war zone. Entering the communication trenches, the rested men would relieve the battle-weary battalions occupying the frontline. Sentries would be replaced, trench stores handed over, orders checked. The return to the front was not the happiest of times.

Opposite: A hospital bed with hospital blues and a soldier's necessaries

Below: Feeding cups for badly wounded or sick soldiers

That night the battalion was going into the trenches again, and last evenings in billets are not generally very exhilarating.

Capt. Bruce Bairnsfather,
Royal Warwickshire Regiment

Right: On leave: gathering belongings for the front

Opposite: Officer's boots for cleaning before returning to the front

HOME

Things all seem unreal & I expect to wake up every minute. I wonder how long it will be before I see you again.

Pte Tom Arnold, France, 1917

Home life was to be severely challenged by the Great War. Mass recruitment meant that many joined in the first months of war, believing in its just cause; many others would be persuaded, and still more emotionally blackmailed. Such peer pressures saw many a man join the colours without due regard to the inevitable consequences for his family if he should be killed, maimed, or otherwise rendered incapable of work. There were great concerns over making ends meet.

Opposite: Back from the trenches

Left: The soldier reunited with his family

I am afraid that father is having an anxious time about non-payment of rents, etc during the war. I have sent him my small bank balance as every little may help.

Lt A.J. Fraser, France, 3 January 1915

With so many men in the armed forces, tensions soon arose between those who were serving in uniform and those who were working to feed the guns, or to keep the wartime economy active. Soldiers all too quickly became disillusioned with the people at home, whom they viewed as being detached from the reality of their experiences of the war, certainly as long as the homeland was not under direct attack. Shortages at home were often reported and found their way into letters destined for the frontline soldier; with the diet of the average Tommy being at most very mundane, there was little sympathy, though his letters show an understandable and touching concern for the well-being of his own family. With the introduction of conscription in 1916, and the emergence of the conscientious objector, there would be divergence of opinion as to the rights of individuals to object to military service. And with industrial unrest over working conditions leading to strikes in 1917, there was even more disquiet, fuelled by the popular press.

Britain was one of the most industrialised nations, its empire built on the back of this prowess. The Midlands could boast to be the workshop of the empire, but with the need for manpower transferring to the armed forces there was soon a crisis in employment: soldiers alone could not win a war. Skilled workers would be required to help feed the guns, build the ships, forge weapons. In the face of peer pressure to join the colours, maintaining the level of skilled workers was no mean task – especially as, in some cases, up to 40 per cent of the workforce had joined up. The poverty of munitions available to the troops was to come into sharp focus during the 'shell shortage' scandal of May 1915. Lord Northcliffe's *Daily Mail* reported that the failure of Sir John French's offensive at Neuve Chappelle in March was due to inadequate artillery preparation before battle, with few shells and a prevalence of 'duds'. The *Daily Mail* laid the responsibility squarely at the door of Lord Kitchener and the War Office. There was truth in the allegations; with the War Office relying on a pre-war system and using existing factories, simply increasing orders was not going to satisfy demand. The scandal caused the Liberal Government to fall; the coalition that followed creating the Ministry of Munitions in May 1915, and appointing David Lloyd George as prime minister in July.

The Munitions of War Act that followed in August 1915 brought all munitions manufacturers under the control of the new ministry. By 1918, it was directly managing 250 government factories, and supervising 20,000 more. There was a bewildering array of types: National Filling Factories (NFF), National Projectiles Factories (NPF), National Shell Factories (NSF), and a whole host of industrial sites concerned with the myriad aspects of trench warfare. While just 500,000 shells were produced in 1914, in 1917 some 76 million were manufactured. In all, some 2.5 million men would work in munitions factories during the war – but this was still inadequate. New sources of labour would be required, and the government turned to the unions in order to implement what would be termed 'dilution' of the skilled workforce – the use of unskilled male labour, and women.

Prior to conscription, men had been encouraged to register as 'War Munitions Volunteers', a status that exempted them from military service – at least in the short run – but required them to be mobile.

'Tommy's sisters': women who fed the guns

Female war work volunteers had been sought in March 1915, yet take-up of the volunteers themselves by the factories was slow at first. They were viewed with some suspicion by many male workers, and agreement had to be reached between employers and unions. The first agreement was attained in November 1914, followed by a variety of others leading up to the adoption of the Munitions of War Act in 1915. With this in place, further negotiations would follow to allow women to take on more and more work in what were traditionally 'closed shops'.

With these moves, and with an increasing number of men being 'combed out' of war work in order to take their place in the frontline, women would

Food supplies were challenged by the German U-boat campaign

increasingly be called to the munitions factories as 'munitionettes' or 'Tommy's sister'. Munitions included everything from the filling of shells to the manufacture of boots, bandages and tents, and an estimated female workforce of 800,000 would be employed in all aspects of their creation, some 594,600 working under the aegis of the Ministry of Munitions in one role or another. Of these, the largest proportion, almost 250,000, would be engaged in the filling and manufacture of shells (the remainder would help create ordnance pieces, rifles and small arms ammunition); they would work with chemicals and on the myriad devices needed in trench warfare. In many cases, women would come to outnumber men. At the huge national filling factory at Gretna, there were 11,576 women employed, almost 70 per cent of the workforce, making cordite, nitroglycerine and other explosives.

Munitions work was long and hard, but women were attracted to it for a variety of reasons, whether from patriotic duty or simply a desire to better their lives. Most were from working-class backgrounds, but there were also others from richer backgrounds who desired the opportunity to 'do their bit' for the country. Some women were mobile, housed in YWCA hostels or lodgings, with canteens set up to cater for them and welfare systems in place. They were also reasonably well paid, typically £2 2s 4d a week; yet this was still half that paid to men – there would be a long way to go before equal treatment.

The question of food was to become a major one during the war; with Britain so hopelessly dependent on imports (up to 60 per cent of its food stocks), it was vulnerable to attacks on its supply system. Early on in the Great War, food control was unheard of, and it was not until 1916 that there was a move towards some form of formal restrictions on consumption. At the outbreak of war, concerns over shortages among the middle and upper classes led to widespread hoarding. That other unholy act, profiteering, was also a major preoccupation of the newspapers, and the opportunity to make money from decreased supply was perhaps too good to miss for some retailers. Both actions were loudly condemned in the press, yet rationing was not to be enacted until 1917.

Imperial Germany was intent on starving Britain into submission, U-boats targeting any ship – neutral included – that might represent a lifeline for Britain in terms of food supply. Around 300,000 tons of shipping were sunk a month; in April 1917 alone, a record 550,000 tons of shipping were lost. This level of destruction meant that some foodstuffs were going to be in short supply. It would also lead to a backlash against those shops bearing Germanic names – with riots and looting prevalent in 1915.

Not until December 1916 was there a specific government department – the Ministry of Food – to deal with such issues. Set up in the wake of concerns over profiteering and hoarding (rather than the bite being taken out of imports by the action of U-boats), this body replaced the Cabinet Committee on Food Supplies that had been created to ensure that there were adequate supplies of the most important foodstuffs. The fact soon dawned that the U-boat menace was a critical one, and the ministry set about persuading the nation that some restraint would be needed. A Food Controller (Lord Devonport at first, then Lord Rhondda) was also appointed, to 'promote economy and maintain the food supply of the country', as well as to increase production and reduce food waste. People turned to growing their own food.

Ida was growing vegetables in our garden, instead of flowers, and we had new potatoes, peas, etc for dinner from the garden all the time I was home!

Pte A.E. Ferguson, France, 1917

Exports of food were prohibited, and a raft of sub-committees and commissions were charged with keeping prices down and ensuring supplies were adequate. Food prices increased steadily through the war, and gave rise to numerous recurring charges of profiteering. Indeed, prices of most commodities rose by 50 per cent during the war, others much more so. Fresh meat would increase by some 100 per cent (imported, frozen meat almost twice this); fish by almost 200 per cent; sugar 250 per cent; and fresh eggs by 400 per cent. Some form of fair distribution system was needed.

With real demand, and little or no home-grown sources, the supply of sugar was a real problem. As much as 70 per cent of the pre-war supply derived from sugar beet grown in Germany and Austria, the rest coming from far-flung British colonies dependent on a transatlantic shipping trade. With the U-boat campaign biting deep, shortages became acute. Sugar was the first commodity to be rationed on a national basis and, in July 1917, householders were issued with ration cards that entitled them to a ration of ½lb of sugar a week.

Sugar was one thing, but the supply of meat was quite a different matter. With much meat imported from the Americas, getting hold of even the cheapest cuts was difficult. Weekly household meat consumption would fall from 2.36lb to 1.53lb by the end of the war. With stocks running low, shortages began to hit hard – and queues at butcher's and grocer's started to lengthen. The War Savings Committee tried to institute 'Eat Less Meat' days in 1916 to assist and the nation turned to fish, the inevitable demand driving fish prices up. Offal was another alternative. Supplies of wheat also started to run dangerously low in April 1916, following the failure of the wheat harvest the year before. Food prices began to rise, and steps were taken to persuade people to voluntarily reduce their intake of bread, with the Royal Family taking the lead in promoting reduced intake.

With 1917 a particularly hard year on the Western Front, and no sign of a breakthrough, people started to fear that the war would never end and that the country would start to run out of food. Panic buying and hoarding reasserted itself, and food control committees started to examine any evidence of waste, from throwing rice at weddings to the size of the offerings in teashops. It was obvious that rationing would have to be extended.

Opposite: Rationing was first introduced in 1917

Left: Making ends meet was a difficult task for many families

In the densely populated region of London and the Home Counties food supply was a major concern, and the London Food Committees were the first to ask for the rationing scheme to be expanded. Early in 1918, 10 million people were the first to receive two ration cards each, entitling them to a weekly ration of meat and fats (butter and margarine). The householder was to register with a supplier, and would then be granted a ration based on cancelled coupons per week. By 1918, typical weekly rations included 15oz of meat, 5oz of bacon, 4oz of fats, and 8oz of sugar. With rationing, food queues gradually subsided, and ration books became commonplace.

Each retailer was guaranteed a supply, and the registered householder would have to queue at the shop. It is estimated that around 1.25 million people queued each week outside shops for their ration. To guarantee supply, just as a customer was tied to a retailer, so the retailer was tied to a wholesaler, and the wholesaler to the importer – assuming that the ships could make it through. In addition, the government set up a system of National Kitchens in June 1918, supplying a range of simple but wholesome foods – and decreasing waste through catering en masse. For some upper-class women intent on doing their bit, working in such establishments, or 'canteening', became a craze.

While on leave, Tommy would have seen many changes besides rationing, not least the growth in war savings advertising. Prosecuting a world war was costly, and ensuring that there were sufficient funds

THE TANK BANK, "NELSON."

Right: A Tank Bank advert

Opposite:
Flag sellers in London

in the coffers led the government to appeal for war savings from the public. The purchase of National War Bonds and War Savings Certificates was portrayed as a patriotic duty, allowing the money to be used in the development and construction of the materiel of war.

Many novel approaches were adopted in promoting war savings, none more so than the 'Tank Banks' that toured Britain in 1917. Following the debut of two Mark IV tanks at the Lord Mayor's Show in London during November 1917, the government mobilised examples of these new 'wonder machines' to raise money and support from the sale of National War Bonds and War Savings Certificates. Six Mark IV male tanks, *Egbert* (No. 141), *Nelson* (No. 130), *Julian* (No. 113), *Old Bill* (No. 119), *Drake* (No. 137) and *Iron Rations* (No. 142), were to tour Britain in 1918, raising millions of pounds through 'Tank Bank Weeks'. Each tank became the focal point for donation. Postcards, tank moneyboxes and other memorabilia were produced in commemoration. With the war's end, those boroughs that had raised the most money received a full-sized tank, usually displayed in parks and squares.

There were other appeals for public money, and flag days became a phenomenon of the war. Flag sellers, usually women, sold small paper flags in aid of charity – and there was a bewildering array of them throughout the war. There were flags in aid of war relief in France and Belgium, and in support of Allies such as Russia and Italy. There were flags to provide comforts for prisoners of war, or for wounded soldiers – usually on specific dates, the flags bearing the words 'Our Day' and depicting smiling soldiers in hospital blues. With the financial burden of supplying soldiers' huts at home and close to the front, there were also special 'Hut Fund' days for the YMCA, Church Army and others.

With soldiers reporting some alienation from the home front and the cushy life there, it came as a shock to most when Britain found it could be attacked directly. The first attacks came from naval bombardment of East Coast towns in late 1914. The assault was not limited to bombardment from ships, however, and the next phase would be the use of airships – Zeppelins. The first aerial attacks were approved by the Kaiser himself in January 1915 – though at first excluding London – with night raids that were intended to target military installations on the Thames estuary. The raids soon escalated. The first successful one came on the night of 19 January, when two Zeppelins attacked East Anglia with high explosive bombs and incendiaries, killing four and injuring sixteen; it was the shape of things to come. London was admitted as a target in February. Though early attempts were ineffectual, at 23.00hrs on 31 May 1915, Captain Linnarz of Zeppelin *LZ.38* dropped the first enemy bombs – some 3,000lb of explosive – on the capital. Seven people were killed and thirty-five injured. The response from the ground was weak, with no aircraft to meet it, no guns fired at it, no searchlights trained on it.

Raids on Britain continued into the summer, though the short nights were a problem for the Zeppelins, which depended on the cover of darkness. Anti-aircraft defences were still ineffectual. Though the pencil-like shape of the airships was often caught in searchlights, the problem was that neither anti-aircraft fire nor aircraft were able to intercept the high-flying airships. In all there were twenty raids in 1915, with 37 tons of bombs dropped at a cost of 181 lives and 455 wounded. Under the threat of aerial assault – as well as periodic spy scares and anti-German riots – the government turned to an Act passed in 1831, allowing the raising of Special Constables. As unpaid volunteers, the Special Constables at first wore only civilian

Opposite: Collecting artefacts from destroyed Zeppelins was popular, and some were sold for charity

Left: Flags in support of the Hut Funds

Below: Charity flags in aid of wounded soldiers

clothes augmented by a duty armband and decorated truncheon; but from 1916 they were issued a dark-blue uniform with peaked cap. Their roles were varied: guarding vulnerable points (including reservoirs against poisoning), patrolling the streets, giving warnings of air raids (and announcing their end), and assisting the public during these raids.

Men of the Royal Flying Corps were seen as heroes on the home front

That 'Special Constable' business would suit me now it would be like having a holiday, *some people have all the luck. Still I suppose Ray Young can't be physically fit or else he would be called up.*

Pte Mostyn Stephens, Warwickshire Hussars, 1917

The clamour for a more effective active home defence led to the army taking command in early 1916. It deployed 271 anti-aircraft guns and 258 searchlights in the hunt for raiders, with ten home fighter

squadrons equipped with newer aircraft and with new ammunition – a mixture of explosive, incendiary and tracer bullets. The Zeppelin raids continued into 1916, with larger numbers of airships targeting London and other cities in the eastern part of the country. The largest raid was on the night of 2 September. It was to be a turning point, as on this night Lieutenant William Leefe Robinson became the first pilot to shoot down an airship over Britain, the rigid-bodied Schütte–Lanz SL.11. Robinson fired three drums of ammunition into the airship, which quickly caught fire and was sent to earth as a fireball, the crew killed outright. This event was to become celebrated, and fragments of the stricken craft were sold to aid the Red Cross; a memorial to the event can now be seen at Cuffley in Hertfordshire. Leefe Robinson was awarded the Victoria Cross, but would later be shot down in France and spent the rest of the war in a prison camp before tragically succumbing to the influenza pandemic at the end of the war.

With Zeppelin attacks losing their effectiveness, the Germans planned a new phase of aerial attacks for 1917, employing large Gotha G. IV bombers in daylight attacks. A new air unit, the so-called *Englandgeschwader*, was formed to carry out the attacks, based near Ghent, in Belgium. The first attack on the capital was intended to be on 25 May 1917, but poor weather meant that the bombers attacked Folkestone and the army camp at Shorncliffe, resulting in sharply increased fatalities compared to those received during the Zeppelin phase. The first effective attack against London was also the deadliest; on 13 June 1917 there were 162 deaths in an attack that also killed forty-six children – most of them under 6 years old – at an elementary school in Poplar, East London.

Further raids saw casualties mount, with the next, on 7 July 1917, seeing civilian deaths from falling anti-aircraft shells (103 recorded falling by the London Fire Brigade), with fifty-four killed overall across the City of London. There would be eight daylight raids in all before improvements in air defences – with the creation of the coordinated London Air Defence Area (LADA) – which caused the Germans to abandon daylight raids, prescient of another war to come. Night raids would recommence on 4 September 1917, with the effects of the first raid evident in the blast-scarred monument of Cleopatra's Needle, on London's Embankment. One of the most tragic raids took place on 18 January 1918, in the attack on Long Acre in Covent Garden, where a single 300kg bomb killed thirty-eight people. The Germans pitted still larger aircraft against Britain with the 'Giant'; one of these was to drop a 1,000kg bomb on Chelsea during a raid on 16 February 1918. The raids continued until the last, and largest, of the war: on the night of 19 May 1918, when thirty-eight Gothas and three Giants attacked the capital; seventy-two bombs were dropped over a wide area of London, but at a cost of six aircraft lost to the air defences and a seventh destroyed on landing.

You will want to know how we got on last night. Well! Very well. It seems that Kentish Town got it very hot, but of course no details are in the papers yet. We heard 3 big bangs which we thought must be bombs bursting somewhere.

Letter to soldier, 20 May 1918

This would spell the last of the Gotha raids, and the last of the attacks on the mainland of Britain – until the Blitz of 1940–41.

AFTERMATH

Aren't you excited? Hurrah! Hurrah! Hurrah! News reached here that <u>peace is declared</u>. Children excited. Thanksgiving service <u>tonight</u>. Whole day's holiday tomorrow!

Postcard, 11 November 1918

At home, enthusiasm for the war was to dim as the years rolled on. Nineteenth-century images of the gallant 'Thin Red Line' in the Crimea, the relief of Mafeking, and the defence of Rorke's Drift must have in part fuelled the initial fervour for the war, the rush to the colours of August–September 1914. But by 1917–18, with the reality of conscription, the daily news of casualties on all fronts, and life on the Home Front becoming an experience of shortages, air raids, rationing and other challenges, the 'new adventure' of the Great War was to become mired in the mud of Flanders.

Yet, for many the end of the war came abruptly. The Central Powers had been crumbling during the

Opposite: Houses decorated to greet returning soldiers

Right: Welcome home

autumn of 1918. Bulgaria was first to capitulate, on 29 September; the Ottoman Empire followed on 30 October, Austria-Hungary on 3 November, and finally Germany herself on 11 November. The terms of the Armistice with Germany required the cessation of hostilities at 11 a.m. on 11 November, along with the evacuation of occupied territory, the surrender of large quantities of arms and equipment, and the disarming and internment of the High Seas Fleet. German soil was to be occupied west of the Rhine. For those troops not instructed to take on occupation duties, demobilisation could not come soon enough. Many men had been discharged unfit, but for able-bodied men, there was nothing for it but to bide their time. Amongst the enforced military discipline, there were also moments of light relief, concert parties, sports days, and the like. It would take many months to return Britain's citizen army back to its peacetime occupations.

The First World War officially ended with the Armistice of 11 November 1918, after a succession of hammer blows fell on the German Army after the opening of the Battle of Amiens on 8 August 1918 – the beginning of one hundred days of continuous advance. During this advance, the Allied armies pushed the Germans back to a line that was broadly similar to the one they had first met the British 'Old Contemptibles' at, four years before. With the

Private Albert Howard died of wounds in October 1918, aged 18

Opposite: The memorial plaque to Pte Wheatley of the Yorkshire Regiment, killed in action in 1915

The British Empire suffered over 900,000 dead, and more than 2 million wounded. In all, at least 10–15 per cent of those who joined up were killed – and twice that for men from Scotland. The Scots were not the only group to lose heavily; with large numbers of middle-class men joining the colours in the early years, there was a disproportionate number who had died: almost a quarter of them. Many would serve as officers, and officers would lose more in proportion than ordinary soldiers. This would be the 'Lost Generation' that would be much discussed and argued about in post-war years, the flower of British youth – for though it is true the majority returned, a large proportion were scarred in some way by their participation in the war. For the next of kin of those who had given their lives in the war, there would be a memorial plaque that resembled an oversized penny – earning it the nicknames of the 'death' or 'dead-man's' penny – some 1,150,000 plaques were produced. Many more men would be seriously wounded, maimed or psychologically damaged; for these men, adjusting back to family life after the war would be a struggle.

Some twenty years after the end of the war, estimates of the casualties recognised some 12,000 amputees, and a further 90,000 with disabled limbs; there were 10,000 blind or visually impaired and 11,000 with hearing impairment; 15,000 had head injuries; and over 40,000 suffered from wounds that still caused active pain. Some 14,000 men still received treatment for wounds that had not healed, with 2,000 servicemen still in hospital two decades after the war. In addition, there were 200,000 suffering from disease brought on by the strain of service and 31,000 men were suffering from shell shock. There is no wonder that the effects of the Great War lived on for decades after the Armistice.

Armistice agreed, the guns fell silent on the Western Front, and the British Fourth and Second Armies commenced their advance into Germany as an occupying power on 17 November. The news of the end of the war was received in many ways – for the soldiers, its occurrence was almost a matter of fact; the entry in Pte Frederick Walker's diary was typical in stating simply, and without drama: 'Armistice signed with Germany'. The popular newspapers, such as the *Daily Mirror*, were to make more of the occasion.

HAM PALACE.

with my grateful people
ending you this memorial
a brave life given for others
in the Great War.

George

HE DIED FOR FREEDOM AND

ROBE
WH

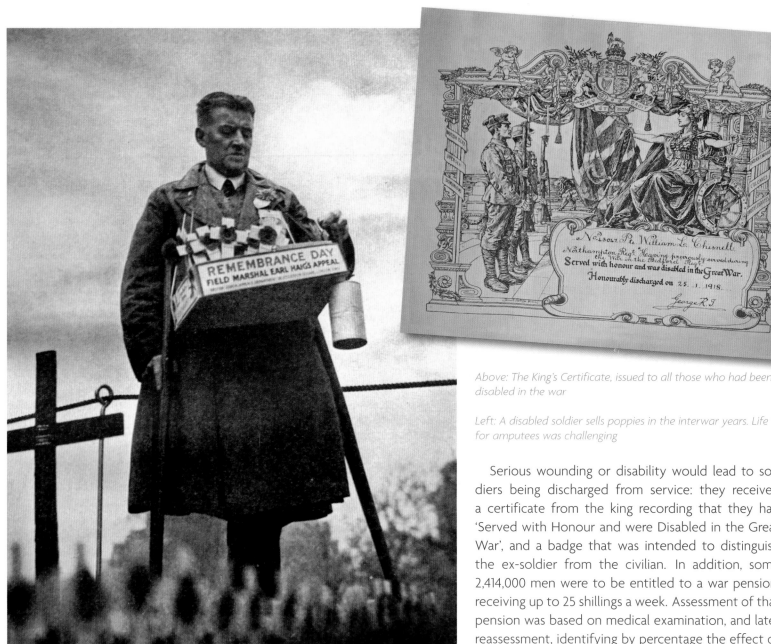

Above: The King's Certificate, issued to all those who had been disabled in the war

Left: A disabled soldier sells poppies in the interwar years. Life for amputees was challenging

Serious wounding or disability would lead to soldiers being discharged from service: they received a certificate from the king recording that they had 'Served with Honour and were Disabled in the Great War', and a badge that was intended to distinguish the ex-soldier from the civilian. In addition, some 2,414,000 men were to be entitled to a war pension, receiving up to 25 shillings a week. Assessment of that pension was based on medical examination, and later reassessment, identifying by percentage the effect of the disability.

For most wounds received in action the cause was evident, but for those injured by accident, establishing whether injuries were obtained during service of the king was subject to continued scrutiny. Take the case of Private George Muckle of the Northumberland Fusiliers, a soldier destined never to serve overseas. He enlisted in 1915, but was kicked by a horse a year later and fractured his leg. Severely injured, he was discharged, though his pension entitlement was considered moot. However, his case was reviewed by the Ministry of Pensions in 1922, who sought evidence from old comrades before granting a pension of 12 shillings a week for life, a disability rated at 30 per cent, a result of war service. Other soldiers would be less fortunate.

First initiated in September 1916, the Silver War Badge was the visible evidence that a serviceman had served his country honourably and, through sickness or wounding, had been discharged from service. Numbered uniquely to the man it was issued to, the badge was proudly worn, and was a common sight on the lapels of all who had been honourably discharged. By the end of 1919, 1,902,016 badges had been issued. Sadly, in Private Muckle's case – a man who, having never served overseas, was not entitled to any medals – his badge and a limp were the only visible evidence of his service to his country.

Pte Muckle of the Northumberland Fusiliers was discharged as unfit due to a broken leg; he was 30 per cent disabled by his war service and received a pension for just two years

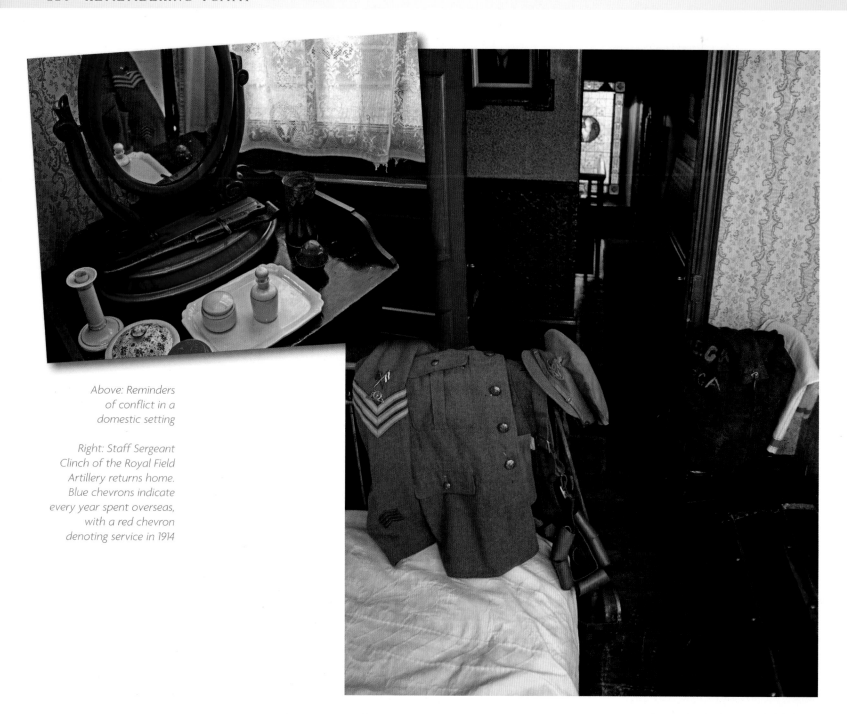

Above: Reminders of conflict in a domestic setting

Right: Staff Sergeant Clinch of the Royal Field Artillery returns home. Blue chevrons indicate every year spent overseas, with a red chevron denoting service in 1914

Demobilisation was available for some men from the end of November 1918, but many more would have to wait some time for their 'ticket', with around 2,750,000 men processed by August 1919. Despite this, demobilisation was not formally complete until 1922. Delays in being released from the army was to cause many frustrations – especially when so-called 'key men', deemed to be essential for economic development, were released first. In some cases, this system was abused, and with this abuse came unrest on both sides of the channel, which the government had to act quickly on in order to avert the spread of mutinies.

I couldn't very well tell you before owing to the censorship but the chaps at No 10 cut up rough over the slow demobilisation. We had a General down to enquire into things & eventually he got us all shipped over to Blighty as hospital patients.

Soldier's letter home, 13 January 1919

For the average soldier, the process of release was complex. Men leaving the army overseas were sent to one of the many dispersal centres where their paperwork would be processed. Allowed to keep their greatcoat and boots, and often their uniform as well, soldiers were also issued with an allowance for new clothes. The issue of several official forms completed the process. Any arrears owed were paid (itemised on the 'Soldiers Demobilisation Account' form), a travel pass was issued, as was a guarantee of unemployment benefit of up to 24 shillings a week: the allowance was to last twelve months (as indicated on the 'Protection Certificate'). The 'Certificate of Employment' was intended to act as a bald statement of what the soldiers had been doing in the army; whether it was of any value to potential employers remains to be seen. Finally, despite demobilisation, the army took pains to point out that each soldier was transferred to a reserve – the nation could still call upon them again in times of need.

In early 1917, soldiers and sailors who had been discharged from the army were mobilising in another arena: the political one. The Military Service (Review of Exceptions) Act of 1917 had suggested that, despite their sacrifices, discharged men could be re-examined and returned to service. It is not surprising that this was poorly received. With an unwieldy title, the Liberal-leaning National Federation of Discharged and Demobilised Soldiers and Sailors (NFDDSS) was set up by ex-servicemen to oppose the concept, and alongside others such as the Labour-linked National Association of Discharged Soldiers and Sailors (NADSS), and the more Conservative, and attractively titled, 'Comrades of the Great War'. The Comrades in particular, open to all, was concerned with the support of its members, but also to 'perpetuate the spirit of fraternity and harmony which characterise the brotherhood in arms'. Together, these organisations fielded around thirty-six candidates for the 1918 General Election representing what was loosely known as the 'Silver Badge Party', named after that distinctive mark of the discharged soldier. Just one candidate was elected: Major Robert Hewitt Baker (formerly of the Lancashire Fusiliers), in Sowerby, West Yorkshire, but seven others attained second place. Amongst the millions who took part in this election – the first in Britain to grant women a vote – were returned servicemen and women, and the families of the deceased, all of whom demanded recognition for their sacrifices, and security for the future. They were to exert a powerful influence.

In calling the election so soon after the Armistice, the fiery and eloquent war leader David Lloyd George was determined to return to power and, having delivered victory, to now deliver the peace. At a meeting in Wolverhampton on 25 November 1918, he made a speech that set out a pledge for a new premiership: a pledge by which he would be forever judged.

What is our task? To make Britain a fit country for heroes to live in … I cannot think what these men have been through. I have been there at the door of the furnace and witnessed it, and saw them march into the furnace. There are millions of men who will come back. Let us make this a land fit for such men to live in.

Western Morning News, *25 November 1918*

Lloyd George promised better conditions for all: better housing; better transport; labour for all, including those women who had toiled in the munitions factories and on the land; and he promised that he would emulate the comradeship of the trenches in order to deliver on his promises. It was a bold commitment.

Opposite: Comrades of the Great War

Gunner Shellis, who had served in France from 1914, was present at the breaking of the Hindenberg Line in 1918. He was discharged after being wounded at the end of the conflict

Opposite: George Eames, 'the soldier baritone', blinded on the Somme

The 'Seal of Honour', the government's scheme for companies to take on war-disabled men

Amongst those due to vote in the election of 14 December 1918 were servicemen still in uniform, a powerful component in a 'khaki election'. Under the Representation of the People Act of February 1918, women over 30 were granted a vote for the first time. This increased the electorate to more than 21 million people, with over 43 per cent of them women; women would have outnumbered men if their voting age had been set lower. Together, then, women and returning soldiers built an expectation that the new world would be a better place, and that soldiers who had served in a war that had touched three continents would return to jobs and housing.

Yet ultimately, Lloyd George's campaign promises would turn out to be hollow. At least 6 million men

had served in the war; almost a million lay in the fields of France, Flanders and other theatres; and then there were those who had suffered some form of disability, half of them permanently. With Lloyd George re-elected on his promises, those who returned at least expected a decent living – yet the post-war world was to be a hard one. With so many men demobilised, and in the depth of a post-war slump following the gearing of a nation for 'total war', finding employment was a nightmare task.

For those disabled, there were even fewer choices available. On 8 September 1919, the king issued a proclamation 'charging employers to engage disabled sailors and soldiers and ordering the names of employers who do so to be inscribed on the King's National Roll'. To achieve this, *The Spectator* reported, 'One place in twenty in any establishment should be reserved for a disabled man, and that employers fulfilling the condition would be permitted to use a special-design; with the words "National Scheme for Disabled Men", on their business notepaper.' That design – soon dubbed the 'Seal of Honour' – would be used everywhere by companies keen to demonstrate their commitment to the returning war wounded.

Nevertheless, for severely disabled men, the situation was bleak. One estimate suggests that some 90 per cent of men who had lost limbs in the war were unemployed in the immediate post-war period. To support them, a charity, the Limbless Ex-Servicemen's Association (LESMA) was set up; its work continues to this day.

For those blinded, St Dunstan's provided a lifeline. Arthur Pearson, proprietor of the *Evening Standard*, set up St Dunstan's as the Blinded Soldiers and Sailors Care Committee in 1915. Pearson was himself blind, and believed that, given training, servicemen who

had lost their sight during the war could have their lives transformed and be able to live independently. His organisation, based in Regent's Park in London, helped give hope to those who had been blinded, and was funded by charity, donations and the sale of cards – its successor still works today. But there would be other disabled ex-soldiers, like George Eames, 'the soldier baritone', blinded on the Somme, who would have to find their own way in the new world and eke out a living as best as they could.

For Tommy, returning home from the war was often an alienating experience, and those who survived and were discharged to a 'brave new world' often found life hard and unrewarding. The cost had been high, and in many cases, soldiers who had served their country well were left without work or a stable home, forced to see out their days selling matchboxes or scraping a living. As one historian wrote:

> *The land fit for heroes turned out to be a land in which heroes were selling bootlaces and matches in the streets, going with their families into the workhouse and tramping the heedless countryside in a vain search for work.*

The road to recovery was a long and arduous one.

REMEMBRANCE

The sale of films, souvenirs and photographs must constitute one of the principal industries of the new Ypres. In most of the battlefield towns you find manufactured souvenirs, but nowhere in such profusion and variety as here. The output of facsimile cartridges bearing the arms of the city, must be enormous; but these are only one class of the astonishing array of articles bearing the single, eloquent word, 'Ypres'.

H.A. Taylor, 1928

At the end of the Great War, old soldiers had little to show for their efforts. The medals of the Great War, mean in comparison with the galaxy of campaign stars issued for the Second World War, fall into just two possibilities: stars for early participants – the 'Old Contemptibles' of 1914, and the men who followed in 1914–15 – and from then on, for the men who served from 1916 onwards, just two simple awards, the War Medal and Victory Medal. The silver War Medal has been described by some experts as 'uninspiring', and the Victory Medal 'like some of the cheap coronation medals handed out to children'. Nevertheless, old soldiers would wear these with pride, though others would never take them out of their boxes of issue. In the hard times of the 1920s and 1930s, those down on their luck would find that these hard-won items would have little intrinsic value, and be difficult to pawn.

Dependent on their hometown, returning soldiers might receive recognition of their service through the local issue of certificates, commemorative medals or books. As early as 1916, the local newspaper *Craven Herald and Wensleydale Standard* planned a memorial for those men and women who had served and died in the Great War.

A record is being compiled of every brave soldier who has paid the price for his patriotism, and who enlisted from the district of which Skipton forms the capital. The work will be illustrated by photographs; will contain portraits and brief biographies of the many officers who have died on the field of battle.

Craven Herald and Wensleydale Standard, *6 October 1916*

The resulting book, based on appeals in the newspaper and on the backs of ration book and sugar cards, was typical of many others across the country, as the nation sought to thank the living and remember the dead. Others received cetrificates to mark their participation, such as that given to Private Robinson of Northumberland: 'Presented by the People of Belford and District to J.T. Robinson, in grateful recognition of gallant services rendered in the Great War 1914–1918'. It was little enough thanks for his loyal service on the Somme. This would be emulated up and down the country.

Opposite: 'Pip, Squeak and Wilfred': the three medals of the Great War

Some good employers had guaranteed jobs for those returning, many others were not in a position to make such grand gestures. In such cases, the unemployment allowance provided by the army was vital. The London County Council, a huge employer, was also to commission a special record of every one of its employees who served in the armed forces, producing a book that was given and inscribed to each employee who had served. One presumes that they were also offered employment, but many others would not be so fortunate – and this would cause great hardship.

In France and Flanders, with the war over, the people returned to find their towns destroyed and their farms devastated. Picking a living amongst the ruins, farmers tried to clear their land, and rebuild what was possible on the old frontline. Soon, the British men and women of the Great War were drawn back to the battlefields: old soldiers to see the fields of their endeavours and to seek out their comrades, women and children to mourn husbands and fathers who still lay in Flanders Fields; each was remembering their own Tommy Atkins.

The Imperial War Graves Commission was born from the vision of one man, Fabian Ware. Too old to serve as a frontline soldier, Ware joined the British Red Cross. His service overseas gave him an insight into the scale of the losses, and of the enormity of the task in recording the dead and registering the often-solitary graves for a time when people would one day return to find their sons and husbands. Tenacious, Ware saw to it that there was a special unit, drawn from the Red Cross and the Army itself, to carry out the process of registration. By autumn 1915, Ware had been able to record some 27,000 graves – an addition to the 4,300 that had previously only been identified and logged – and by May 1916 this had risen to 50,000, and

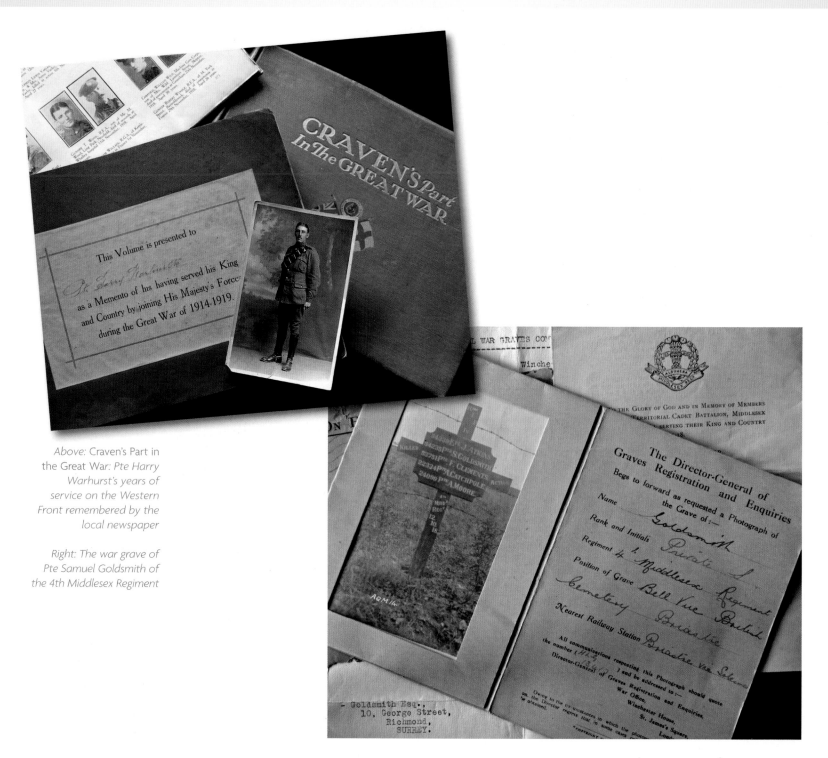

Above: Craven's Part in the Great War: *Pte Harry Warhurst's years of service on the Western Front remembered by the local newspaper*

Right: The war grave of Pte Samuel Goldsmith of the 4th Middlesex Regiment

150,000 by April 1917. In 1917 the Imperial War Graves Commission was born, constituted by Royal Charter, and committed to the care of the war graves of the Imperial forces of all those 'who died of wounds inflicted, accident occurring or disease contracted, while on active service'.

The birth of the Commission saw the establishment of principles that became, in the latter years of war and the early years of peace, hotly contested. Those men and women who died overseas would be buried close to where they fell – there would be no repatriation. Cemeteries would be uniform in style and approach; to avoid inequality, there would be no provision for private memorials, and the State would ensure that no distinction would be made between the graves of the lowliest private and the loftiest general. For some, this was too much. But the Commission stood its ground.

The Commission's decision is that those who have given their lives are members of one family ... and that, in death, all, from General to Private, of whatever race or creed, should receive equal honour under a memorial which should be the common symbol of their comradeship and of the cause for which they died.

Imperial War Graves Commission, January 1918

Five Points CWGC Cemetery, Lechelle, France

In the aftermath of the war, the Imperial War Graves Commission was charged with the protection of over 500,000 graves and more than 1,200 cemeteries in France and Flanders alone. For the farmers to return to their land, isolated graves had to be concentrated in larger ones so that they could be cared for – but in the early years there was disarray. The eminent architect Edwin Lutyens was one of three to be appointed to construct the cemeteries that would become such a focus for pilgrims. Even before the end of the war, Lutyens visited the front to examine the task ahead and found 'a ribbon of isolated graves like a milky way across miles of country ... for miles these graves occur, from single graves to close packed areas of thousands'. Soldiers had to be exhumed from these often hastily dug graves so that cemeteries could be constructed, and special Exhumation Squads were formed from volunteers in the Labour Corps and men who re-enlisted to carry out this vital task. These men sought out the dead of the battlefields, looking for any clues that might give evidence of an identity and so lead to a named headstone. It was a vital task.

With the end of the war, the Commission worked tirelessly to bring order to the chaos of the battlefields. Each cemetery was to be carefully designed and constructed, and each headstone marked the place of burial of soldiers, sailors and airmen. With a uniformity of approach, the headstones bore the badge of the regiments under which the men had marched, and carried their name and rank. Relatives were given the opportunity to add an epitaph, for which a fee per letter was payable – although it seems that this was not always vigorously enforced. For those men who could not be identified, their headstone would bear the carefully chosen words 'An Unknown Soldier of the Great War. Known unto God'. From 1919 to 1921, the Commission's responsibilities grew large, with the construction of cemeteries containing thousands of individual graves, the planning of horticulture, and the raising of carefully inscribed headstones.

Then there were those men who had no known grave. For the Ypres Salient, a monumental stone gateway was planned at the Menin Gate, in the brick ramparts of the city. It was through this portal that every soldier passed, and it was fitting that a monument to this act be constructed at this place. The arch was constructed by Reginald Blomfield and was inaugurated in 1927, its panels listing the names of

Opposite: Five Points CWGC Cemetery, Lechelle, France

Left: A returned watch from Pte Robert Purdie of the Leinster Regiment, killed in action on 12 April 1917. The watch is inscribed with Pte Purdie's name, and no doubt played a role in identifying his body

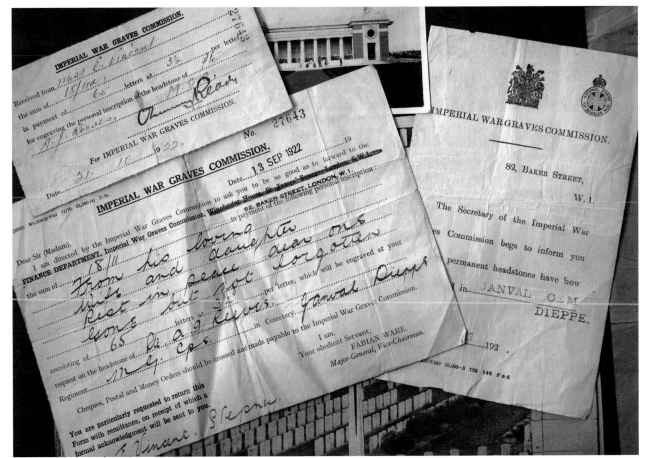

The epitaph for a soldier's grave: an IWGC receipt for payment of 18 November received for the inscription to be added to Pte Reeves' grave

54,395 servicemen who died in the Ypres Salient, but whose bodies were never recovered. Its inscription was 'Here are recorded names of officers and men who fell in Ypres Salient, but to whom the fortune of war denied the known and honoured burial given to their comrades in death'. On the Somme, with its vast death toll, was to be constructed an immense edifice of brick and stone. Designed by Lutyens and inaugurated in 1932, the great monument towers into the sky, composed of a series of stone arches supported by vast square pillars, with room enough for 72,246 names – 'the Missing of the Somme'. It is the biggest monument to the missing in the world.

It was to these cemeteries, graves and memorials that visitors came in numbers in the early years of peace, and then again in the run up to the Second World War. Tentative visitors soon swelled to a throng; in turn enterprising former officers became aware of the possibilities of employment, in a harsh world where discharged 'Temporary Gentlemen' were ten a penny.

Battlefield touring threatens to become popular as soon travel restrictions are relaxed. Realising that the most reliable and interesting guides will be ex-soldiers who have actually lived and fought the various areas. Continental touring organisers are already registering suitable men for service. Many officers have declared their arranging and conducting parties personally.

Yorkshire Evening Post, *19 February 1919*

To support visitors, there were not only willing guides, but also a large number of battlefield guidebooks produced by tour companies, rail companies and others, of varying quality. Those published by the Michelin

THEIR NAME LIVETH
FOR EVERMORE

*Above: Lutyens' Thiepval
Memorial to
the Missing of
The Somme, 2016*

*Opposite: Poppy wreaths
at Blomfield's Menin Gate,
Ypres, 2014*

Company indicate the large numbers of potential battlefield visitors in those early days, with almost 1.5 million copies of their guides sold by the end of 1921. An industry also grew to supply visitors with all types of souvenirs imaginable, but this initial boom in the battlefield-curious soon tailed off in the mid-1920s, only to be revived, with extra vigour, a few years later when Britain was on the cusp of another war. Often the return was challenging for old soldiers, and the old charitable organisations that had helped Tommy survive his time at the front – The Church Army, The Salvation Army and the YMCA – now assisted him and his relatives to return to the devastated area. Some estimates suggest that 60,000 people visited with the assistance of the YMCA, and there would be other charities, such as the St Barnabas Society, which assisted battlefield pilgrims. Back at home, Lutyens' Centotaph, first built in wood before being rendered solid in Portland Stone, became the focal point for remembrance from 1919, and the Tomb of the Unknown Warrior, installed with great reverence in the entrance to Westminster Abbey, marked the nation's sacrifice.

In 1921, The British Legion was born out of four of the main old soldiers' organisations (including the Comrades of the Great War), with Field Marshal Earl Haig its first president. The Legion's principal role

Opposite: Back to the front; battlefield guides to the Ypres Salient

Souvenirs of the 1928 British Legion Pilgrimage

THE LATE EARL HAIG AT BRITISH LEGION POPPY FACTORY.   26173.

Earl Haig at the British Legion Poppy Factory

The Great Pilgrimage of 1928 was monumental in scale. Commencing on 4 August, the symbolic date of the British declaration of war; it was to last until 8 August, the date of commencement of the Allied offensive that ended it. The pilgrims were carried to France by seven ships and were billeted with families, in schools and available barracks. Progressing across France and Belgium, saluting war graves and cemeteries as they went, the former Tommies, their families and those who had lost men in the war met finally at the Menin Gate in Ypres. The Grand Place, now being steadily healed after its wartime destruction, was filled with the pilgrims who formed fours and marched through the town as they had done a decade or more before. Alongside the 11,000 were others, an estimated 50,000 attending to view the spectacle. It had not been so long ago that no one could gather in that open square, in that shell-blasted urban landscape.

On 11 November 1921, the first British Poppy Day was held in Britain on the third anniversary of the end of the Great War. The appeal, known as the Haig Fund, raised £106,000. The origin of the poppy and its association with remembrance has a history that springs from the words of Canadian surgeon John McCrae, and his 1915 poem *In Flanders Fields*, written in the Ypres Salient. McCrae's poem contained the line 'In Flanders

was in supporting ex-servicemen and women, and in raising and administering relief funds for those fallen on hard times. However, the Legion also assisted groups travelling to gravesides and battlefronts for relatives and old soldiers – its greatest ever return was the 1928 Pilgrimage, when it supported 11,000 of its members to visit the sites of battle, to remember what it was like to be a Tommy in the fields of Flanders ten years before.

fields the poppies blow, between the crosses, row on row', a line that was to inspire American Moïna Michael, and French Madame Guérin to adopt the poppy as a mark of remembrance during 1918–19. It was Madame Guérin who sought to manufacture and sell the delicate, artificial poppies across the USA from the devastated areas of France, as a relief to the local population. And in 1921, Madame Guérin's poppies finally made their appearance in Britain, where the concept was embraced by Field Marshal Haig and the British Legion. It was a success, and the British Legion went on to register the design of the poppy so that proceeds from their sale could be used in the support of disabled and destitute servicemen and women. The Legion opened its Poppy Factory in 1922 with just £2,000, to 'give the disabled their chance'. There is a poppy factory to this day.

The poppy has now reached iconic status. With the coming of the centenary of the Great War in 2014, sales of the poppy raised a record £44 million for the Royal British Legion to carry out its charitable mission. The poppy was also chosen to mark the loss of every life from the British Empire in that war, with an installation of 888,246 ceramic poppies in the moat of the Tower of London. The installation, *Blood Swept Lands and Seas of Red*, was devised by the artist Paul Cummins and stage designer Tom Piper, and was named after the first line of a poem by an unknown Tommy that Cummins himself discovered. Each poppy was handmade and each one hand-placed, until a sea of red spread through the moat. It was an intense installation that drew criticism from some art critics, but admiration from the estimated 5 million people who visited the site before it was dismantled by Armistice Day 2014. One segment of it – 'the weeping window' – toured the country during the whole centenary period, 2014–18.

A 1921 poppy from Madame Guérin, 'The Poppy Lady from France', manufactured in the devastated area

But alongside the dead, what of the living? What of the men who returned? Who would remember those Tommies who returned to their land, and who endured?

We're Here Because We're Here was a most remarkable living memorial to the soldier that appeared briefly on the streets of Britain on 1 July 2016. On that day, marking the loss of 19,240 men in the Battle of the Somme, young men in uniform congregated in the streets, stations and shopping centres of modern Britain. For the most part silent, the 1,600 volunteers broke into the soldiers' refrain 'We're here because we're here, because we're here, because we're here; we're here ...' It was an immediate success. Designed by artist Jeremy Deller and staged by Rufus Norris of

Clockwise from right: Poppies of the 'Weeping Window' from the installation Blood Swept Lands and Seas of Red, *at St George's Hall, Liverpool, November 2015;* We're Here Because We're Here, *Newcastle upon Tyne, 1 July 2016 (Jamie Corbett)*

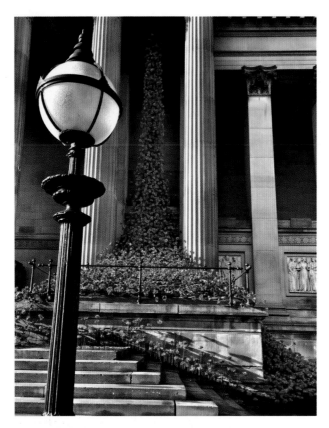

the National Theatre, *We're Here* was one of the most powerful memorials of sacrifice. But arguably, it is the incongruous setting of the silent young men in uniform from another age in the bustle of modern Britain that provided a memory of all those who served, of those who returned and of those who laid down their lives for their country. By remembering Tommy in this way, we will never forget.

ACKNOWLEDGEMENTS

A project as complex as *Remembering Tommy* requires the support of a large number of people in delivering its aims. We have intentionally sourced locations that provide the right feel for the period, and we are indebted to those organisations who have allowed us to use appropriate 'backdrops'. Particularly important to us was the enthusiastic support that we received from Beamish Museum (www.beamish.org.uk), a time capsule set in 1913, in that pivotal year before the onset of war. Jacki Winstanley provided us with access, support and practical advice, and we cannot praise her or the museum too highly. If you have not visited this magnificent resource, set in beautiful countryside in County Durham, you should do so.

Getting the right trenches is clearly important in any book on the soldiers of the Great War. Taff Gillingham and Khaki Devil Ltd (www.khakidevil.co.uk) were exceedingly generous in allowing us free rein to explore their trenches (not open to the public, but a working film and TV location), and populate them with equipment. Fort Nelson (www.royalarmouries.org) was the backdrop to our barracks; situated close to Portsmouth, the Fort is a national museum for artillery, and well worth a visit. The generosity of the Royal Armouries and Joss Loader, and the hospitality of Nigel Hosier were both superb. We thank the National Trust and Rachel Drew for access to the amazing 'Mr Straw's House' (www.nationaltrust.org/mr-straws-house/), an early twentieth-century family house that was maintained by its original residents as a house 'out of time'. The house provided the backdrop to several of our middle-class scenes.

Historical interpreters helped us with some of our photographs, and we commend their dedication to historical accuracy, as well as their enthusiasm and generosity. We thank in particular Keith Bartlett and the Durham Pals (groups.yahoo.com/group/TheDLI/), the able cooks of the 29th Field Kitchen (www.freewebs.com/29thfieldkitchen/) and Peter Zieminski and the men (and machine guns) of the Queen's Own Royal West Kent Living History Group (www.thequeensown.com), particularly member Richard Fisher and his Vickers (www.vickersmachinegun.org.uk).

We are grateful to many individuals in crafting our book. Laurie Milner and Ted Peacock, in particular, opened up their magnificent collections to our admiring gaze and searching camera lenses. Julian Walker allowed us to use his magnificent tabletop and helped us with period set dressing. Generously, several people proffered their time and opinions, and supported us with loans of relevant items and images. We thank Taff Gillingham and Paul Reid for expressing their interest in the project and sharing advice. We are grateful to Jonathan and Ian Jowett, Simon Lomax, Libby Simpson and David Upton for help and advice. German historian Robin Schäffer donated a genuine Iron Cross to the project; Mike Stockbridge loaned us the magnificent image of the British soldier that forms our frontispiece. Several people allowed us to use images in their care, and these have enriched our knowledge and experience and, ultimately, the book: Joan Airey allowed us to use her picture of Frank Ward; Ben McKenzie gave us access to the letters and photograph of Lt Christopher Wilkinson-Brown from his collection; and the Sedbergh School archive kindly granted us permission to reproduce the haunting image of 2nd Lt Hugh de Bary Cordes MC, who died in 1918.

We have also benefited from the knowledge of generous contributors to the Great War Forum (1914–1918.invisionzone.com) and the British Ordnance Collectors Network (www.bocn.co.uk), as well as Geoff Carefoot at Tommy's Pack Fillers (www.tommyspackfillers.com).

Books of this sort are labours of love; ultimately we have relied heavily on the support of our families: for Peter, Julie and James; for Chris, Sari and his sister Sue. Without them, this book might never have seen the light of day.

SELECTED SOURCES

A large number of individual sources, letters, diaries and private papers were consulted to bring the words of the soldiers of the day to these pages, and to help us create what is ultimately an amalgam of the soldier's experience on the Western Front. While many of these are brief – diaries and cameras having been outlawed at the front for fear they might fall into the hands of the enemy – it is possible to pick out an unwritten subtext to many of them. The simple statement 'in the pink' that is often encountered in soldiers' letters conceals the real hardships felt by the majority of men at, or close to, the front. Often, it falls to the more literary soldiers to express their experiences, even if these are mundane. To that end, in addition to letters and diaries we have used a range of books written by soldiers in that most productive ten-year period after the war; a period marked by the outpouring of soldiers' memoirs. We have selected the least well known, perhaps least literary – but the quotes obtained from these express well what can be gleaned from less highbrow letter writers. These sources give voice to the countless thousands who simply 'got on with it', returning to forget. The books listed opposite are the ones that provided the quotes; a great many other primary and secondary sources were used in writing this account.

Adams, B., *Nothing of Importance: A Record of Eight Months at the Front with a Welsh Battalion*, R.M. McBride & Company, 1918.

Anonymous [Bell, D.H.], *A Soldier's Diary of the Great War*. Faber & Gwyer, 1929.

Bairnsfather, Bruce, *Bullets & Billets*. Grant Richards, 1916.

Buckley, Francis, *Q.6.a and Other Places, Recollections of 1916, 1917, 1918*, Spottiswoode, 1920.

Clapham, H.S., *Mud & Khaki*, Naval and Military Press, 2009.

Copping, A.E., *Tommy's Triangle*. Hodder & Stoughton, 1917.

Douie, Charles, *The Weary Road: Recollections of a Subaltern of Infantry*, Strong Oak Press Ltd, 1988.

Edmonds, Charles [C.E. Carrington], *A Subaltern's War*. Peter Davies, 1929.

Empey, Arthur Guy, *Over the Top*. A.L. Burt, 1917.

Ex-Private-X [A.M. Burrage], *War is War*. Victor Gollancz, 1930.

Eyre, Giles E.M., *Somme Harvest: Memories of a PBI in the Summer of 1916*, Naval and Military Press, 2009.

Gillespie, 2nd Lieutenant A.D., *Letters from Flanders*. Smith Elder & Co., 1916.

Hitchcock, Captain F.C., *'Stand To': A Diary of the Trenches, 1915–1918*, Naval and Military Press, 2009.

Lambert, Arthur, *Over the Top*. John Long, 1929.

Rogerson, Sidney, *Twelve Days on the Somme: A Memoir of the Trenches, 1916*, Frontline Books, 2009.

The destination for history
www.thehistorypress.co.uk